APPEAL YOUR PROPERTY TAXES — AND WIN

by
Ed Salzman

Panoply Press, Incorporated
Lake Oswego, Oregon

Cover design: Bruce DeRoos
Art: Janora Bayot

Library of Congress Cataloging-in-Publication Data

Salzman, Ed.
        Appeal your property taxes — and win / by Ed Salzman.
            p.   cm.
        Includes index.
        ISBN 1-882877-01-2 : $9.95
        1. Tax assessment — United States. 2. Tax protests and appeals — United States. I. Title.
HJ3241.S25   1992
343.7305'42—dc20
[347.303542]
                                                        93-6671
                                                        CIP

This book is intended to provide general information. While exceptional care has been taken in researching and verifying the material used in it, be aware that property tax laws change and appeals practices differ somewhat from community to community. If you have legal questions or concerns about your property taxes or tax appeal, consult your attorney.

Panoply Press, Inc.
P. O. Box 1885
Lake Oswego, Oregon 97035
(503) 697-7964

TABLE OF CONTENTS

PART I: WINNING APPEALS

Part I
WINNING
APPEALS

1

The Taxing Process

Should you appeal your property tax assessment this year? If you're like most American property owners, you probably will do the same thing you've done every other time you've received an assessment you think may be too high — nothing.

Most taxpayers think the attempt is futile, that they can't beat city hall. Some probably even fear that an appeal will result in a closer examination of their property and a subsequent tax **increase**. Others may think the appeals board is attached to the assessor's office and thus will be hostile to appellants. Some citizens believe an appeal is too much trouble for the long-shot chance of a small reward. Others simply can't face the trauma of making an appearance before a government board. Some think a great deal of work and possible expense is involved in preparing an appeal.

Why More Taxpayers Should Appeal

In fact, most of this thinking is dead wrong. Many more property owners should appeal. They have a good chance of winning. Even in areas with excellent assessment operation, a substantial percentage of the appellants win reductions, many of them with the recommendation or concurrence of the assessor's office.

Consider these facts: the appeals board usually consists of ordinary citizens refereeing differences of opinion between the property owners and the assessor's office. The board can reduce assessments but normally cannot raise them. Hearings are informal and citizens can submit their cases in writing without the necessity of appearing in person. And the rewards can be substantial. In an area with a $20 per $1,000 tax rate, a $10,000 reduction can save a property owner $200. Furthermore, the value set by the board must in most cases be used by the assessor as the basis for future assessments. So the benefits keep accruing over several years.

Looking at Your Tax Bill

From the taxpayer viewpoint, the process starts each year with an unwelcome notice — the annual property-tax bill. Among other things, the notice usually lists any changes in taxes and assessments from the previous year, how the proceeds are distributed, the tax payment options (if any) and a legal description of the property. Most jurisdictions also include a separate sheet describing the taxpayer's appeal rights or include this information on the basic form.

The tax bill may come as a shock, especially in areas where voters have approved ballot measures requiring significant reductions in property taxes. These reductions have not always materialized in areas where property values have been escalating rapidly. In some areas, taxpayers expecting reductions actually received hefty increases because there happened to be a hot real estate market at the time. In most of the nation, real estate prices stabilized or actually dropped during the recession that started the 1990s.

The notification system varies greatly from state to state. In some states, taxpayers receive their notices of assessment — the value placed on their property by the assessor — long before the actual property tax bill is mailed. This gives the property owners the opportunity to appeal any assessment increase before the taxes are due. In other states, however, the assessment and tax bill are combined into a single notice that arrives only a short time before the payment is due. In these instances, the appeal cannot be heard until after the bill is paid, and those who win reductions through the protest process are entitled to refunds. In some areas, separate notices of assessment increases are mailed only to those property owners who receive substantial increases.

Know Your Appeal Rights

The appeal rights of the taxpayer are usually provided with every notice of assessment. It is invariably written in government language that doesn't exactly encourage citizens to take advantage of their rights. Cut to the basics, it tells property owners where to write or call to obtain petitions for the filing of appeals with the appeals authority, which may be called a Board of Assessment Appeals, a Board of Equalization or some such name.

Every year, many thousands of property owners pay more than their fair share of taxes because they fail to appeal their assessments. Why is this the case? Isn't the appraisal system fair and scientific? The answer is that it is reasonably fair and fairly scientific, but it is far from perfect. Here, in a nutshell, is how an assessment is calculated for each parcel of property each year.

The Assessment System

In an ideal world, hordes of expert assessors would leave the assessor's office on the day chosen as the theoretical date of assessment and inspect every piece of property in the county or other taxing jurisdiction on that one day. (The date is January 1 or July 1 in most areas, but there are some deviations.) Assuming all these assessors were using the same strict standards and applied them evenly, few taxpayers would have any grounds for complaint or appeal.

But in the real world, that isn't even close to what happens. If an assessor's office is doing its job according to the law, each parcel is subjected to a physical inspection only every few years. The elapsed time between visits runs from three to 10 years, depending on the area. Theoretically, this means that once every few years, an appraiser is supposed to make a detailed inspection and evaluation of every piece of property. But the appraiser often arrives at a time when no one is home (except perhaps a large and unfriendly dog), and the evaluation is based on a walk around the grounds and a few peeks inside the windows. In addition, many citizens exercise their right not to allow the appraiser inside their homes.

After the inspection is concluded, the field assessor computes a new value for the property and places that in the record jacket for each parcel. (That jacket normally includes a detailed description of each parcel, notations from all visits, and computations showing how each assessment was reached. Record-keeping systems vary tremendously from jurisdiction to jurisdiction, with some totally computerized and others still keeping records by hand.) However, there is usually a time lag between the date of inspection and the date of assessment. During that time, which could be as long as a year, the real estate market could undergo major changes. So the assessor's office applies a "trend factor" to each parcel, an adjustment up or down that supposedly reflects market action during the elapsed time.

This system of trending is also used during the remaining years in the appraisal cycle. As a result of this procedure, at no time is a parcel's assessment based strictly on a physical appraisal. Every year, it is subject to the whims of the trending statistics.

Bucking the Trend

It is impossible to comprehend how each assessment figure is reached — and thus the rationale for most appeals — without an understanding of the trending system. In a nutshell, here is how it works:

Every county or other taxing jurisdiction is divided into neighborhoods based on the historical movement of real-estate values. Every year, all real-estate transactions within each neighborhood are broken down by type of parcel (bare land, single-family home, apartment building, etc.) and by purchase price. A sales "array" or list shows how many parcels sold above and how many sold below the previous year's assessed value. From this array, three averages known as the *median,* the *arithmetic mean* and the *weighted mean* are often used by the assessor to indicate changes in real market value over the previous year. This change factor or trend is then applied to every parcel in that category in that neighborhood.

The arrays themselves show that the system contains imperfections. Some parcels that sold below assessed value could get assessment increases if a majority of properties were appreciating in that neighborhood. By definition, the use of means, averages and medians creates inequities. But this trending system is an accepted method of assessment and is used throughout the nation despite its built-in unfairness. The alternative — annual analysis of every single parcel — would be so expensive that it could virtually bankrupt the taxing jurisdiction.

Trending: One Good Reason to Appeal

Government officials recognize that the trending system is far from perfect. That's why the assessor's proposed trends each year are subject to review in many states by one or more review authorities, which may be a statewide agency or a local citizens panel or both. The local review board in some areas can hire a professional appraiser to study the proposal. The trends become final only after the review process is completed and the assessor has dealt with any changes recommended during the review process.

Because this trending system is based on averages, it cannot take into consideration a variety of factors that can have a marked effect on the value of a home — location within a community, how well the property has been maintained, architectural features that make one home more desirable than another, the attractiveness of the grounds and all the intangibles that make the value of some properties move at a faster rate than others.

The use of this trending system is the fundamental reason why more taxpayers should appeal. Yet, very few appeals can be won simply with an attack on the trends used by the assessor. That's because most appeals boards have already studied the trends and found them statistically justifiable — on average. In order to win an appeal, the taxpayer must find an approach that establishes a value for the particular parcel that disproves the trended average value used by the assessor.

Every appeals board should understand the imperfections in the system and stand ready and willing to grant reductions to those who present strong factual cases before the citizen panel.

Watch Your Appeals Board in Action

While the ground rules for successful tax appeals remain the same no matter which board is hearing your appeal, the chemistry of every appeals panel is different. Evidence and arguments that will produce a whopping reduction before one board will not fare as well before another. For that reason, the prudent petitioner will try to learn as much as possible about the tendencies of the board.

Some petitioners spend a few hours or even a few days wathcing a board in action to learn what documents, mathematical analysis and arguments sway those particular board members. Is the board apt to be influenced by a sob story based on the hardships thrust upon the peririoner by ever-increasing property taxes? Does the board automatically grant reductions based on a recent purchase price or a professional appraisal? Does the board respond better to an agressive or a mild-mannered presentation?

In some areas, it is possible to talk with board members in advance and ask them what evidence they like to receive. In other jurisdictions, assessors are willing to provide information on the tendencies of the local board. It may prove possible to check with others who have filed appeals and learn from their experiences. Although all boards are supposed to base their decisions on hard evidence of property value, the human element cannot be eliminated. And a sound evaluation of that human factor can be the difference between the success or failure of an appeal.

The remaining chapters will provide taxpayers with several strategies designed to optimize their chances of winning property-tax appeals. The advice is based on many years of experience watching government in action, on interviews with property-tax administrators throughout the nation and on observation of thousands of hearings conducted by appeals boards.

The Arithmetic of Property Taxation

The following chart, presented in simplified form for ease of comprehension, shows how assessors calculate the trend factor applied to every parcel of the same type in the same neighborhood. This kind of "sales array" is used in all years that a parcel-by-parcel physical appraisal is not conducted.

TREND FACTOR CHART			
Parcel Number	Sales Price	Assessed Value	Percentage Difference
1	$40,000	$60,000	67
2	60,000	66,000	91
3	140,000	150,000	93
4	80,000	85,000	94
5	160,000	168,000	95
6	32,000	33,000	97
7	196,000	196,000	100
8	100,000	100,000	100
9	72,000	69,000	104
10	200,000	190,000	105
11	50,000	47,500	105
12	425,000	400,000	106
13	107,000	100,000	107
14	76,000	70,000	109
15	55,000	50,000	110
16	125,000	100,000	125
17	60,000	40,000	150

This chart shows that, of the 17 properties listed, six sold below assessed value, two at assessed value and nine above assessed value. To ascertain the proper trend figure for this neighborhood, an assessor might be expected to apply a series of mathematical tests, with the following commonly used:

The *median:* This is simply the middle sale in the list. As can be seen in the chart, sale number 9 was at 104, or 4 percent above assessed value.

The *arithmetic mean:* This is the average of the numbers in the percentage column at the right, in this case 103, or 3 percent above assessed value.

The *weighted mean:* This figure is determined by adding the sales-price and the assessed-value columns and then establishing the ratio between the two (by dividing the assessed value into the sales price). In this chart, the ratio is 104, or 4 percent above assessed value.

These calculations would be used by the assessor in determining the changes in assessments for all properties in that category (bare land, homes, apartments, etc.) within that neighborhood. In this instance, the assessor would probably select a ratio of 104 and increase the assessments on all parcels by 4 percent. Just a glance at the chart will show that the use of such a trending figure will result in those at the top of the list paying more than their fair share of taxes and those at the bottom less than their fair share. The owners of parcels 1 through 8 certainly would have grounds to appeal, as would any other property owners who could make a convincing case that their parcels likewise are worth less than the assessed value. Assuming that this chart reflects the market in the neighborhood, almost half the property owners in that area might be able to win an appeal.

California: The Great Exception

The much heralded passage of Proposition 13 in 1978 gave Californians a substantially different property-tax assessment system than the rest of the nation. In California, each year's assessment does not reflect the market value of the property because Proposition 13 established a maximum assessment increase or 2 percent a year, regardless of the trends in the real-estate market.

However, every parcel in California is subject to revaluation at true market value when the ownership is transferred. This can and does result in the owners of two identical and adjacent parcels paying substantially different amounts of property taxes. The United States Supreme Court has validated this inequity, stating that the "doctrine of acquisitional value" is a legitimate method of levying property taxes.

For Californians, this means that the first notice of assessment following the purchase of a parcel is especially important. If the assessment exceeds the price paid for the property or its real market value, the taxpayer should appeal. An unfairly high valuation in the year of acquisition will otherwise be used as the foundation for taxation so long as the parcel remains in the same ownership.

2

The First Steps

Believe it or not, many property owners — especially those who have lived in the same home for many years — don't have the foggiest notion of the actual market value of their land and buildings. Most people are primarily concerned about the property-tax burden, and if taxes rise precipitously in any given year, then they howl and take a closer look at the tax bill.

The prudent property owner will examine the property tax bill in detail every year to see whether the change in the assessment appears justified. Does the assessment seem reasonable, based on recent sales of similar properties in the neighborhood? One easy way to check is to determine the asking prices of properties currently on the market in the neighborhood. They are usually advertised in the classified sections of local newspapers. Another is to ask real estate brokers familiar with the area to offer opinions of the value of your property.

If the assessment established by the county assessor looks high, the next step is to check the assessor's records to determine how the assessment was established. Was a physical appraisal made of the neighborhood in the previous year, or was the assessment increase based strictly on statistical trending? Before going to the assessor's office, make a list of other properties in your neighborhood that are similar to yours. Then check the assessor's records to determine whether these neighbors also received the same increase. While at the assessor's office, you may also obtain a list of recent property sales in your area. Check them to make sure the sales justify the level of increase imposed by the assessor.

Even if this check of the records and recent sales turns up no convincing evidence of an over-assessment, the trip may be worthwhile. One of the most common grounds for a reduction is an error in the assessor's records. The diagram of the house may be inaccurate, resulting in an mistake in square footage. The records may list too many bathrooms or fireplaces. You may be charged for an outbuilding, such as a woodshed or barn, that has been removed from your land.

Also, the assessor may not be aware of any major problems with the property that have developed since the last physical reappraisal. These can be the basis for a reduction. Often it is possible to bring these matters to the attention of the assessor's office and resolve the issue without a formal appeal. In some areas, however, that is not possible because of the short time span between the establishment of the tax roll and the payment of taxes.

The Basic Rule

If you even think your assessment may be high, file an appeal. You have nothing to lose except a little time. In some counties, an appeal automatically triggers a detailed review of the property file. Quite often, errors are found to the benefit of the taxpayer. In that event, the assessor should recommend a reduction to appeals board.

There are a variety of strategies that can be employed to seek a reduction in an assessment and thus in property taxes. They will be discussed in detail in the next chapter, and they include:

- Errors in the assessor's records.

- Recent sale of the property for less than assessed value.

- Property currently on market for less than assessed value.

- Property valued at higher amount than comparable neighboring property.

- Property valued too high, as evidenced by recent sales of comparable property in the neighborhood.

- Property value reduced by special factors, such as limited use or adverse location.

- Property value reduced because of exceptional depreciation.

Whatever the approach, it is important that the appeals procedure be carried out properly. Otherwise, it is possible to lose an appeal simply because the proper procedures were not followed. Let's take a look at the basic guidelines.

Using the Printed Form

Although the law may not require that a special printed form be used for an appeal before an appeals board, it usually does require that the petitioner put specific information in writing. In order to guarantee that these requirements are met, the best bet is to obtain a standard appeals form from the clerk of the board, the assessor's office or other such source. Forms and procedures vary from area to area, but the basic principles are the same. Usually, the appeal rights notice that is mailed with each tax bill provides the address and telephone number of the board clerk.

When filling out the form for transmission to the clerk's office, make sure it is complete and accurate. If it is deficient, the clerk probably will return it to you. And if it is inaccurate, the board might infer that you are being less than candid, and that could prejudice your case.

The most commonly used form is one applying to vacant land, residences and business buildings. In some jurisdictions, a separate form is used for personal property, such as tools and equipment used by businesses.

The real-property petition normally contains only a few items, but the form isn't always comprehensible to the ordinary citizen because it tends to use technical language. The following items are usually contained on the appeals form:

Description of the property in question: The basic rule is to use the information listed on the tax bill. That would include such items as the name of the owner, the tax year, the assessor's account number, the map and lot number, the street address of the parcel being appealed and the assessed values listed on the tax statement.

Reduction sought: Some place on the petition is a line requesting the petitioner to establish a value for the property. The petitioner must be prepared to justify whatever number is used for the market value. It will do little good simply to use the previous year's assessment and state that there was no justification for an increase unless the property owner is prepared to show that the real-estate market was absolutely flat for a year.

What's an *improvement*? The language of assessment is not always easily understood by ordinary citizens. Perhaps the single word that creates the most confusion is "improvement." In assessor language, an improvement is a building or other structure placed on a piece of land. Some jurisdictions make it easy for citizens by simply using the word "buildings," but many states and localities insist on using "improvement." As a result, petitioners often file appeals based on the assumption that they are being charged for recent alterations to their property because that is their understanding of the word "improvement."

Petitioners should also be aware that the term *land* does not necessarily refer to naked land but can also include so-called site improvements, such as the hookup of water and sewage to a home and whatever excavation may have been required to prepare a site for construction.

Unfortunately, the assessment system frequently requires that the value of each parcel be divided between land and buildings. This is a headache for everyone involved in the process because properties are normally valued as a single unit in the real world, not as separate land and building elements.

Generally, it doesn't pay to appeal the land portion of the bill because the assessors usually value all land in a neighborhood similarly. Unless there is some specific reason to protest the land value, put the reduction in the buildings (improvements) and into the total. Also, make sure the arithmetic on the appeal form is accurate because you could make a mistake that will work against you.

Case Study*: A Tale of Two Sales

Facts:

Lester Andreson and Norman Chipp both bought homes in the Weeping Willow subdivision in the same month, close to the date used by the assessor for valuation. Andreson paid $189,000 for his property, and Chipp's purchase price was a bit lower at $187,000. Both parcels were appraised at $205,000. Both Andreson and Chipp appealed, claiming that the proper assessment was the purchase price. Andreson opted not to appear before the board, submitting only a deed

* **NOTE ABOUT THE CASE STUDIES:** The facts presented in each case study are based on actual hearings before an appeals board. There is no change in the outcome of the appeal or the reasoning by the board. Only the names of the petitioners have been changed, and in some cases the details have been simplified for ease of comprehension.

showing the price he paid for the property. Chipp appeared before the board, presented several documents relating to the sale and answered questions from the members.

Decisions:

Chipp received a reduction in his assessment, to the purchase price of $187,000. Andreson's assessment was left at $205,000.

Reasoning:

The board refused to take Andreson's deed at face value, especially after receiving information from the assessor that Andreson bought the property from a friend and that the house was never exposed to the real estate market. Chipp presented evidence that his parcel had been bought on the open market, that the home had been available through a multiple listing service for several months and that a real estate commission had been paid. The board decided that Chipp's purchase price reflected true market value, while Andreson may have received a bargain.

Personal appearance: The form usually asks whether the petitioner wishes to appear at the hearing in person or juste submit the case in writing. If you can present an air-tight case in writing, there is no need to appear. The board will give you just as much consideration as those who do appear. But in most cases, the petitioner should be present to answer questions from the board and to rebut any evidence presented by the assessor. In some areas, a representative of the assessor's office attends all meetings. In others, the assessor presents a written recommendation. In yet others, the board receives no arguments from the assessor and bases decisions on evidence from the petitioner and a study of the files on each parcel.

Truth in petitioning: One section of the form may provide background for the board on such matters as the date and price of purchase, offerings for sale, independent appraisals, and additions to the property. On the surface, this information may not seem important, and many petitioners either leave it blank or use guess-work to fill in the blanks. Many an appeal has been lost because this section has not been completed accurately.

Example: A petitioner bought a home for $119,000 in May 1988. Three years later, he appeals an assessment of $162,000. Rather than look up the accurate date and pur-chase price, the owner says in the petition that he paid $115,000 in 1989. The board looks at the assessor's re-cords, which have accurate purchase information, and finds the discrepancy. What does the board conclude? That the petitioner was bending the truth to present a more dramatic case. The appeal goes down the drain. The best bet is to complete all sections of the form accurately since misinformation can hurt more than the truth.

The case for a reduction: The most important section of the form allows the petitioner to provide the basic reason why relief is being requested. This space should be used for a succinct statement describing which rationale the petitioner is using as the basis for a reduction. It is not advisable to try to cram all the details of the appeal into a small space. The details should be presented in as concise a manner as possible on a separate sheet of paper.

The signature: The bottom of the form usually includes a line for the signature of the owner and the address where correspondence should be mailed. In some states, it is important that a power of attorney be filed if someone other than the owner or a close relative will appear.

The deadline: Make sure the petition is filed by the deadline noted on the appeal form. Normally, at least one month is allowed between receipt or publication of the assessment notice and the deadline for filing. No excuses are accepted for late filings. You will be notified by the clerk when and where your appeal will be heard

by the board. You'll find that notice and deadline procedures vary greatly from state to state, so it is important
to be aware of the appeals deadline in your community.
(See chapter 8 for details of appeals procedures in your
state .)

3

Grounds for Appeal

One way or another, a successful appellant must make a convincing case that the assessor made a mistake in placing a value on a specific piece of property.

The fastest way to lose an appeal is to vent frustration with high taxes and launch a written or verbal attack on government officials. Believe it or not, boards of appeal do not want to hear about property taxes. They don't want to see tax bills or tax records. They don't want to hear about hardships caused by high taxes (although there are rare occasions when hardship might help). Boards want to hear about assessments and market values of specific properties in specific neighborhoods.

Another fast way to lose an appeal is to present statistics that apply to the nation, a region, a state or even a metropolitan area. General economic conditions and housing prices do not constitute just cause for assessment reductions. The case must be based on conditions applicable to the specific property under appeal and others in the same neighborhood, as defined by the assessor.

This chapter will chart the various ways that a successful appeal can be crafted. It is usually not advisable for more than one or perhaps two of these approaches to be attempted in an appeal because the try-everything strategy is likely to make board members think they are getting a snow job.

The successful appeal is specific. The petitioner requests a reduction to a specific amount and justifies that request with evidence that applies to that specific parcel and that specific neighborhood. One basic rule: A petitioner should know what the property would bring on the open market and why. Many an appeal has been lost because this exchange took place at the appeal hearing:

> **Board member:** *"Do you have any idea what your home would bring if you were to place it on the market today?"*

> **Petitioner:** *"I'm not interested in selling. I have no idea."*

If you have no idea what the property is worth, you do not have adequate grounds for appeal. Remember this: In the absence of strong evidence from the appellant, the benefit of doubt goes with the assessor in most jurisdictions.

That having been said, keep in mind that board members are human. They are supposed to be unemotional and operate under guidelines set down by state officials. If you can use your powers of persuasion to make a board sympathetic to your point of view, you might be able to win a reduction even though the technical merits of your appeal may be somewhat shaky.

What follows are the avenues of appeal that are most likely to succeed.

Assessor's Record in Error.

As mentioned previously, the easiest way to get a reduction is to find an error — in your favor — in the assessor's records. When these errors are found, and they must be consequential, the assessor usually agrees to a reduction and the tax saving is essentially automatic. In some cases, the assessor can grant a reduction administratively, making a formal appeal unnecessary.

Some assessors routinely check the records of every parcel under appeal and often find errors that surprise the appellant. In other jurisdictions, the taxpayer must find the errors by examining the file in the assessor's office and checking it carefully.

Here are some of the errors that can produce an assessment reduction:

Square footage: The size of a building is an important consideration in the establishment of value. For a variety of reasons, it is possible that the assessment is based on the assumption that a home or other building is larger than it is.

Keep in mind that assessors use a rough method of measurement, and the assessor's square footage will rarely be identical with the figures used by a property owner. A small difference will not be grounds for a reduction.

Assessors usually measure a building from the outside and round off inches to the nearest foot. If you use this system and find the assessor's square footage high, you might have a valid claim for a reduction. In many cases, the assessor's office will send an appraiser to the property to double check the measurements.

Special features: Assessments are based in part on how many bathrooms, fireplaces, built-in kitchen appliances, decks, and other features are contained in a home. If the assessor is, in effect, charging the property owner for an excessive number of these items, a reduction may well be in order.

Classification: The value of a home depends, in large measure, on the construction classification placed on the property by the appraiser. The system can vary from state to state, but the basic principle is the same. In Oregon, for example, a 1-to-8 rating system is used, with 1 representing a residence that is barely habitable, while 8 is an elegant home with expensive architectural detail. (Some homes are even rated 8-plus if they are considered top-of-the-line mansions.)

It is difficult for the ordinary citizen to determine the proper classification for a home by studying the standards set down by government officials. But a homeowner can check the classification of similar properties in the neighborhood to see whether a reasonable pattern seems to have been established. Some homes have never been entered by an appraiser, and that can lead to misclassification.   Or perhaps an inconsistent judgment call was made by an assessor many years ago. In any event, if you suspect that your property is over-classified, request an inspection by the assessor's office. You will either get a lower classification — and thus a reduction — or an explanation for your classification.

Construction progress: Assessments on buildings under construction are normally based on the percentage completed on a specified date each year. On occasion, the assessor's records show a speedier rate of construction than actually took place. By presenting detailed construction records, it may be possible to get the assessor to recommend a reduction. However, it should be noted that any such reduction will apply only to that year.

Incomplete buildings are red-flagged by the assessor's office for annual physical inspection.

Recent Sales Price

Is there any better evidence of the value of a piece of property than a recent sales price? Probably not. Yet a petitioner would be making a mistake to think that a reduction is automatic if the sales price is lower than the assessed value.

Petitioners often present a deed showing a date the property was transferred and the sales price — and they still lose their appeals. How can that happen?

Simple. The petitioner must present the "right" evidence to show the board the date on which the buyer and seller agreed on a price, not the date on which the final papers were filed. The petitioner should also satisfy the board that there were no unusual arrangements to the sale, such as an exchange of property, and that the sale resulted from true arm's-length negotiations.

The most useful document the petitioner can present is the so-called "earnest-money agreement" that is signed by the buyer upon making an offer for a parcel of property. This agreement tells the board when the deal was struck, whether a real-estate broker was involved and exactly what price was agreed upon.

The date is important because the usual valuation procedure calls for a "trending" from the date of sale to the assessment date, ordinarily Jan. 1 or July 1. Let's assume the property was bought for $100,000 on April 15, real estate values in the neighborhood were increasing at a rate of 12 percent a year, and the assessment date is July 1. A proper assessment would be $102,500, the purchase price plus 1 percent a month for the two and a half months between April 15 and July 1.

Because property values are based on open-market transactions, a board will look askance at a sales price if the property was only on the market for a few days, if it was not offered through a real-estate broker, if it was not made available through the multiple-listing service, if the sale was between relatives or friends, or of there was anything else unusual about the deal.

To an ordinary citizen, it may seem wrong for an assessment to include a 6 or 7 percent real-estate brokerage commission. But most states have determined that in order to establish uniformity, it is assumed that every sale is accomplished with the standard commission (which is often lower than 6 or 7 percent in the case of large commercial and industrial properties).

Let's assume that a petitioner bought a home assessed at $110,000 through a private party for $100,000 without benefit of a real estate agent but the seller marketed the property aggressively with signs, newspaper advertisements and other means. Let's assume further that the home was on the market the previous year through a broker for $100,000 but there were no offers on the property. On the surface, it appears that $100,000 is a proper assessment. Some boards might agree, but a more likely outcome would be an assessment of $106,000 or $107,000, equivalent to the purchase price plus a 6 or 7 percent real estate commission.

In general, an appeal based on a recent purchase price has the best chance of success. But that is only the case if there was nothing unusual about the purchase and the proper documentation is presented. A petitioner should not assume that just one sales document will be sufficient. A board member might want to see the contract with the real estate agent, the earnest-money agreement, the closing statement and the deed. All pertinent documents should be on hand in case someone challenges the normalcy of the sale.

Property Currently on Market

Another relatively simple way to win a reduction is to present evidence that the property owner is willing to sell the parcel for less than the assessed value. By far the best evidence of that willingness is a contract with a real estate agent to offer the property for a price below assessed value.

It is not sufficient for the owner to post a "FOR SALE" sign on the front lawn. Nor is it sufficient to print flyers and place a classified ad in a weekly newspaper. The board wants to be assured that the offer is legitimate and that the property has been marketed aggressively for a reasonable period of time (not simply for the two weeks before the hearing).

In other words, the board must be convinced that the price is based on a sincere effort to sell rather than a ruse to get a property-tax reduction.

Expert Opinion of Value

Taxpayers frequently attempt to obtain assessment reductions by presenting evidence designed to show that the assessor's appraisal does not reflect the realities of the real estate market. In effect, the petitioner is challenging the trending statistics compiled by the assessor's office but is making a case based on one specific parcel of property in one sub-neighborhood.

On occasion, this approach will work. But success requires the preparation of a careful statistical analysis that cannot be shot down by recent sales trends in the neighborhood.

If you think this is the best approach for you, remember that you will not succeed with a general attack on the trending system and the sales data used by the assessor to compile the changes to the annual assessment role. A much narrower line must be drawn.

Many petitioners base their cases on evidence provided by a real estate agent familiar with the neighborhood. The agent signs a letter stating what the house might bring on the market and finds some recent sales to back that opinion. On the surface, it appears that a board might be convinced by such a case. Perhaps some new and naive board member might buy it, but most board members know that almost everyone has a friend in the real estate business who will write a letter and find sales that will back a specific position. So this kind of evidence from a real estate broker is usually discounted heavily if not rejected altogether.

More weight is carried by a so-called "fee appraisal" prepared by a licensed appraiser for a fee of several hundred dollars, more than most petitioners are willing to pay. Most appraisals are done for lenders as part of a mortgage investigation. Appraisals are also conducted for a variety of other purposes, including some for the assessment appeals hearings.

A fee appraisal includes a detailed description of the property and what it would cost to build. The heart of the appraisal is the comparison of the subject property with three or more comparable parcels — known in the trade as "comps." In order for an appraisal to carry weight on appeal, these comps must be truly comparable to the subject property — in size, year of construction, architectural features, construction qualification and neighborhood. Too often appraisers use comps several miles from the subject property. Ideally, the comps should be on the same street or at least on the same assessor's map.

In recent years appraisers have been working overtime as a result of the reduction in the cost of mortgage interest. Property owners by the droves have refinanced their mortgages, and each time the lending institution ordered an appraisal to make sure that they were not being asked to lend too much money on a parcel.

As a result of this activity, boards have been inundated with petitioners claiming that their assessments exceed the values established by licensed appraisers. These citizens think they have a right to demand that their assessments be lowered to the value set by the appraiser for the lender. After all, these are certified experts who presumably know at least as much as the bureaucrats in the assessor's office.

Do these appellants automatically get their reductions? No. It didn't take these assessors and boards of appeal long to see a disturbing pattern in these appraisals. They ran consistently below mortgage value, while appraisals ordered for initial mortgages following the sale of a parcel produced more realistic valuations.

How did this situation arise? Very simply; the word spread within the appraisal community that lenders wanted conservative refinance appraisals to produce an extra margin of safety in the wake of the nation's savings-and-loan crisis. Appraisers can't afford to anger lenders or they'll be out of business. As a result, the typical refinance appraisal in 1992 ran 5 to 10 percent below true market value. The courts have recognized that two appraisals, both done in good faith by experts, can vary as much as 10 percent. So the appraisers can take the conservative approach without risking the loss of their licenses.

Astute members of appeals boards learn how to analyze appraisals and find flaws that invalidate them for assessment purposes. One common flaw is the use of comparable sales that are more than six months old. Another is underestimation of the value of the land. And a third is the use of an unrealistic dollar amount in making adjustments for differences in square footage.

A sound appraisal can be instrumental in winning a reduction, but the use of a flawed one essentially dooms an appeal. A property owner would be better off compiling a self-appraisal than resting a case on a deficient appraisal. How does an ordinary citizen compile an appraisal? It isn't as difficult as it seems in an area where there is an active real estate market. (This approach will not work if there are no recent sales of similar properties in the neighborhood.)

The first step is to obtain, from the assessor's office or a real estate broker, a listing of all recent sales in the neighborhood. (In some areas, there are companies that sell computerized lists showing sales and assessed values.) The next step is to identify **all** sales of reasonably comparable properties in the neighborhood, with special emphasis on those in the immediate proximity to the subject property. This list should include the date and price of sale, the assessment, the size of the property, the construction classification, and any other information that might show comparability. Don't try to compare a 4,000-square-foot class 3 home with a 2,000-square-foot class 7.

It is important to list all comparable sales — not just those that buttress your case — because the board will have the list of sales and will not be favorably impressed with a highly selective presentation that includes only favorable information. If it turns out that a significant percentage of the truly comparable properties sold below assessed value, the inference can be drawn that the subject property has also been overvalued by the assessor. The key to success is the drawing of a clear picture for the board that shows a pattern of overassessment for your type of home in that neighborhood.

CASE STUDY: Size Makes a Difference

Facts:

Luther Miller lived on a two-acre parcel in a rural area about 25 miles from a large city. After receiving a 15-percent assessment increase (and a $300 boost in his tax bill), he decided to see whether he could find sound grounds for an appeal. He went to the assessor's office and checked the valuations for all his neighbors. As it turned out, most of his neighbors lived on parcels that ranged from five to 15 acres. Miller did some simple calculations and came to the conclusion that his land had been assessed at about $17,000 an acre, while the value placed on his neighbors' land ranged from $8,000 to $13,500 an acre. He filed an appeal, demanding that he be assessed at the same per-acre rate as his neighbors.

Decision:

The board rejected Miller's request for a reduction.

Reasoning:

The board explained to Miller that he did not go far enough in his research. The standard assessment procedure in that area was to designate one acre of a parcel as a "home site" with a relatively high valuation. The valuation of the remainder of the land depended on the size of the lot, with the per-acre value declining as parcels grew larger. The board told Miller that he was not making a fair comparison when he placed the same per-acre value on his small plot as he did for his neighbors. Studies show that the value of land diminishes as larger parcels are offered for residential purposes.

Unfairly Assessed With Neighbors

The previous approach was based on an analysis of sales. This type of appeal is based on a comparison of assessments in the neighborhood without regard for market value.

Keep in mind that the appeal will be brought before a board charged with assuring that no taxpayer assumes more than his or her fair share of the burden. Irrespective of market value, a board will attempt to assure that property owners in each neighborhood get similar assessments for similar property.

In preparing an appeal on these grounds, it is vital that the comparisons be limited to the immediate neighborhood of the subject property and that there be no significant differences in the classification of the property, square footage and other important comparative information. It is important to analyze land and improvements (buildings) separately because lot size, location and view can account for a large difference in assessments.

Appellants commonly seek reductions based on comparisons with neighbors who have different size homes or lots. This approach is flawed because generally speaking, the larger the home or lot, the lower the value per square foot or per acre. Assessors, by the way, often work from tables showing the rate of decline in value of bare land as the size of the parcel increases. Another factor can have a bearing on the valuation of a large parcel of bare land — the separate assessment of a "home site" from the remainder of the property. This "home site" of perhaps one acre will carry a much higher value than the remainder of the land.

CASE STUDY: Can Do for Condos

Facts:

Virginia Mueller lived in a large condominium development in which all units were essentially the same, except that the property was about evenly divided between one- and two-bedroom units. At a meeting of the homeowners' association, Mueller and many of her neighbors discovered that a few of her fellow condo *owners had appealed their assessments the previous year to the County Board of Equalization and had won reductions of $7,000 per unit, a tax savings of about $175 per unit. The following year, Mueller appealed on the ground that all properties in such a homogeneous development should be treated alike.*

Decision:

Virginia Mueller was a granted a $7,000 assessment reduction.

Reasoning:

Recent sales in the condo market showed that the units were selling at the assessed value or close to it, and the assessor urged the board not to grant reductions because of the market conditions. However, the appeals board rejected the assessor's argument in favor of the appellant's claim that the law required that all citizens with identical property be treated alike. In this instance, the board placed its responsibility for equalizing assessments ahead of its responsibility to retain all assessments at true market value.

An appeal based on neighborhood comparisons is especially useful in planned developments where there are several identical units. This includes condominiums and homes surrounding a golf course. It is not difficult in these cases to make sure that the assessor has treated all comparable units equally.

Boards of appeal themselves create opportunities for appeal by granting reductions. If a neighbor receives a reduction for whatever reason, others in the same area might be able to take advantage of the situation if the board action creates inequality of assessment.

CASE STUDY: At the Water's Edge

Facts:

Victor and Suzanne Lewis lived in a house adjacent to a small pond in a suburb of a major city. Homes surrounding the pond were roughly the same in size and character. Most of the properties were assessed in the $300,000-to-$400,000 range, with the bulk of the value in the land because of the highly desirable location. The Lewises discovered, as did most of their neighbors, that a home on the pond was recently sold for $275,000, about $50,000 below assessed value. The Lewises appealed the assessment on their own home, seeking a reduction from $350,000 to $300,000 based on the recent sale of a nearby home.

Decision:

The appeals board upheld the $350,000 assessment and granted no relief to the Lewises.

Reasoning:

The appeals board examined all recent sales of properties adjacent to the pond and found that seven homes had been sold during the previous year. The sale cited by the Lewises appeared to be an extraordinary circumstance because all the other homes sold at or above assessed value. As one board member commented: "One sale a trend does not make."

Exceptional Depreciation

Taxpayers frequently receive assessment reductions by presenting evidence that there are problems with properties that would reduce their market value. Some people refer to this as an appeal based on *deferred maintenance* but that is not quite an accurate term. *Exceptional depreciation* more accurately describes the situation. Understanding the difference is important for anyone preparing an appeal based on physical condition of a structure.

Consider these examples: House number one has a 22-year-old roof that should be replaced, carpets that are almost worn out and walls that could stand a fresh coat of paint. The property owner has waited longer than normal to get the work done — a case of deferred maintenance. Is this property owner likely to get a reduction from the board of appeals? Probably not, even though a good case can be made that the value of the house has been affected by condition of the roof, carpeting and walls. The reason is quite practical. If boards started granting reductions based on the age of roofs, the wear level of carpets and condition of wall coverings, the system would break down completely. Boards generally assume it is the owners' responsibility to maintain their property, and failure to do so should not be rewarded with a reduction.

House number two has a leaking roof, and the result is visible water damage to the living-room ceiling and dry rot in the walls. The foundation also has cracked and there is evidence of termite damage at one end of the house. Will this property owner win an appeal? Probably. Assuming these conditions are listed on the appeal petition, the assessor will probably re-inspect the home to determine the extent of the damage. The assessor will probably then recommend a specific reduction to the board.

The difference between the two houses is the degree of damage. One was the result of normal wear and tear common to all properties. The other was exceptional and would require expenditures beyond what is normal for maintenance of a property.

The key issue before the board in cases of exceptional depreciation is the proper dollar amount to cut from the assessment. It is the responsibility of the taxpayer to provide the evidence supporting a specific amount, and the best way to get that evidence is to have professional repair firms provide written estimates as to the *cost to cure* the specific problems, such as the water damage and dry rot. Horseback guesses and verbal estimates are not sufficient. The board will want to see firm written bids or estimates from legitimate contractors.

CASE STUDY: The Human Factor

Facts:

Hannah Simmons was an 89-year-old widow who lived in an area that had been given a 20 percent assessment increase because homes in the neighborhood became a hot item in the real-estate market. Mrs. Simmons lived in a house — actually, more of a shack — that was built by her husband, who died before he could complete it. She survived on a small pension and couldn't afford to complete construction of the home or even maintain it properly. Even with the increase, the assessment only came to $33,000, far less than most other homes in the area. The assessor placed the Simmons home in the lowest quality category, indicating that the structure was barely habitable. Mrs. Simmons appeared before the board pleading for relief, claiming she could not afford a tax increase. She presented photographs showing the deplorable condition of the property but didn't have any idea what the parcel was worth.

Decision:

The board restored Mrs. Simmons' assessment to the prior level, eradicating the 20 percent increase.

Reasoning:

This was an instance in which the appellant failed to present the crucial evidence of market value, but the board felt that her property was hardly marketable at any price, except perhaps for the land. Board members felt sympathetic for the plight of the woman and leaned over backwards to give her a helping hand. This kind of an appeal does not work very often, but it is most apt to be effective in a situation in which property is in deplorable condition and simple logic tells a board that a large single-year increase is unjustified.

Miscellaneous Special Situations

The preceding are the most commonly used grounds for appeals, but there are several other approaches that also can win reductions if they are properly presented. In all cases, it is difficult for a board to grant a reduction unless the appellant can present specific evidence to support the amount of the reduction requested. What follows are some of the situations that definitely can produce tax savings.

Trending of outbuildings: The "improvements" listed in the assessor's records may include more than the main residential structure. The assessor may also place a value on a greenhouse, a shed, a barn, a chicken coop, whatever. These do not appreciate at the same rate as homes. Indeed, in many instances a strong argument can be made that outbuildings generally depreciate.

In checking the assessor's records, a property owner can easily determine whether the assessment for the new year treated outbuildings the same as the main structure. If so, there is a good chance of winning an appeal. Incidentally, assessors try to take this differential between homes and outbuildings into account, but this goal is not always translated into action.

Unusual lot features: Without going into a complex analysis of how land values are established, a parcel with a site that is somehow less than the norm for the area should be given special consideration. For example, access may be difficult because of the terrain. Some of the land may not be usable for some reason, such as the shape and slope of the lot. Some of the land may be swampy.

If the assessor has not taken these negative factors into account, the property owner might be able to win a land-value reduction. But the evidence must be clear and a strong rationale should be provided for the amount of the reduction requested in the appeal.

Limited marketability: Some properties have been afflicted with problems that make them unmarketable at almost any price. Examples: Toxic contaminants have been discovered in the ground and they must be eliminated. A major landslide has developed and the property is creeping down a hill.

These are solid grounds for appeal, and the real issue is how much of a cut should be made in the assessment. Toxic contamination is now a common problem, and the usual way of handling this situation is to reduce the assessment by the amount it will cost to eliminate the problem. Once the contamination is eliminated, the property becomes marketable and the assessment is increased again.

Some of the other marketability issues, such as landslides, are much more difficult to quantify. In these cases, it behooves the applicant to prepare a detailed case to support a low assessment. (Some states have guidelines for the assessment of property rendered essentially unmarketable by landslide, perhaps with a reduction to one-third to one-half of the normal market value.)

Adverse location or environment: In the previous section, the issue was an environmental problem dealing with the subject property directly. Now we are looking at situations in which properties are adversely affected by factors outside the boundaries of the parcel. A house might be located next to a noisy freeway ramp, an auto wrecking yard, a busy commercial center, a parking lot or some other "nuisance."

Boards of appeal have a great deal of difficulty with this sort of claim. Common sense tells the members that the property owners are adversely affected. After all, the cardinal rule of real estate is that the three most important factors affecting price are location, location and location. On the other hand, boards are often thwarted by the necessity to place a dollar value on the nuisance. The petitioner should try to provide some evidence or at least rationale for a specific amount of reduction, perhaps based on such reductions granted by the assessor or other boards in similar situations elsewhere in the city, county or state.

CASE STUDY: There Goes the Neighborhood

Facts:

Following a long controversy, the city of East Lynn constructed a large water tower in the center of a residential development in the Mount Rose section of the community. Residents claimed that the tower was a blight that had reduced the value of their homes, which had previously been selling in the $150,000-to-$300,000 range, depending mainly on size. Charles and Lorraine Sturm were among numerous Mount Rose homeowners who went before the appeals board to plead for a reduction, claiming that the presence of the water tower devalued their home. The Sturms presented evidence that an abnormal number of Mount Rose homes had been placed on the market and that none of them were selling, whereas there had been an active real-estate market prior to the construction of the tower.

Decision:

The Sturms received no reduction in their assessment, although the board was sympathetic with their plight. The board asked the assessor to maintain a special watch on the Mount Rose area to determine whether a blanket reduction might be warranted in the following year.

Reasoning:

Although the board recognized the potential for value loss from the tower, there was no hard evidence that in fact such a downturn had taken place. The evidence showed that the asking prices of homes on the market were above assessed value, and as yet not a single parcel in the area had sold below assessed value. The board urged the Sturms and others in the Mount Rose neighborhood to keep a close watch on sales and seek relief again should the real-estate market support their contention. (Later in the year, the assessor reported to the board that there indeed had been several recent sales in the area, all above assessed value. The inference might be drawn that the area been underassessed prior to the erection of the tower or that the presence of the tower had minimal effect on home- buyers.)

Unbuildability of land: A common area of dispute between landowners and the assessor is the buildability of a parcel of land. Obviously, a home site is worth a great deal more than a piece of property that cannot be built upon. Assessors assume a parcel is buildable unless there is concrete evidence to the contrary.

The best way to get a piece of land reclassified from buildable to unbuildable — and thus get a whopping assessment reduction — is to present a building-permit denial or similar document showing that the land is unbuildable. A common reason for denial is that a septic tank or other means of sewage disposal cannot be installed on the property. The best evidence is a recent letter from a government agency to that effect. An old denial letter may not be accepted because there have been significant advances in waste technology in recent years.

CASE STUDY: Shock Therapy.

Facts:

For many years, Rex and Charlene Hazzard owned a piece of bare land in a semi-rural area. They inherited the property and at one time attempted to build a home on it. However, their application for a septic-system permit was denied, and the land was considered un-buildable. Year after year, the Hazzards paid a relatively small amount of property taxes on the land, which was assessed at $4,900. The parcel was included in the area subject to physical reappraisal in 1991. When the assessment arrived, the Hazzards almost went into shock. The new assessment was for $60,000, and the tax bill rose in one year from $125 to $1,500 — a 12-fold increase. The Hazzards had received no warning. They asked the assessor's office to provide an explanation for the sudden jump, and they were in-formed that the land was now considered buildable.

Decision:

The appeals board asked the assessor's office to take another look at the property because such a sudden increase did not seem reasonable, especially since it came without any warning. After further review, the assessor recommended a reduction in the assessment to $15,000, which the board accepted.

Reasoning:

Technically, the key issue in this appeal was buildabil-ity. In essence, the burden of proving unbuildability falls on the property owner. The assessor decided that the old septic-system denial was no longer valid be-cause it might be possible to dispose of sewage on the Hazzard property through the use of newer and more expensive technologies. The appeals board expressed concern about the way the assessor's office handled the increase, with the board taking the view that any *stratospheric rise should be discussed with the property owners unless it is part of a trend being applied throughout the neighborhood. At least, the board indicated, the assessor should have given the Hazzards an opportunity to check into the continued unbuildability of the land. The $15,000 figure was tantamount to a holding action, giving the Hazzards time to determine whether a new-technology sewage system could be installed on the property.*

Underimprovements: Assessors are supposed to appraise properties at their "highest and best use" within the zoning restrictions established by the local government agencies. At times, this can create situations in which a building — especially a dilapidated structure — can actually detract from the value of the parcel as a whole.

In this case, the dilapidated building is considered an "underimprovement" and the cost of demolishing and removing it should be subtracted from the value of the land. Anyone with such a building should make sure the assessor has granted such a reduction. Otherwise, an appeal probably would be successful, especially if the petitioner can present the right evidence, a clear showing that the building would detract from a sales price, plus bids or estimates showing the cost of removing the eyesore.

Using the Taxpayer's Worksheet

The following relatively simple worksheet is designed to help a property owner determine whether an appeal based on comparable sales or comparable assessments is likely to succeed. The chart also may indicate how much of a reduction should be sought. Information to complete the chart can be obtained from public records in the assessor's office or from real estate brokers with access to sales and assessment records.

There is no limit to the number of neighboring properties that can be added to the chart. The object is to find a pattern that would support a reduction. In selecting neighborhood parcels for the chart, try to find as many as possible that are roughly the same size, class, age, lot size and amenities as your property. Then compare your assessments with those of the other properties, especially with any of these parcels that recently changed hands.

TAXPAYER'S WORKSHEET

	Your Property	Neighbor 1	Neighbor 2	Neighbor 3
Address and assessor's map number				
Square footage of home				
Proximity to appellant's property				
Construction class				
Age of home				
Size of lot				
Unusual features				
Assessment				
Sales price (if recently sold)				

4

Other Types of Property

$\mathbf{T}$he vast majority of petitions brought before boards of appeal involve either single-family homes or bare land. But there are several other classes of property, and it is possible to appeal assessments on mammoth factories, small mobile homes and a mechanic's tool chest. Here is a brief description of other categories of property and the key points in the appeals process.

Mobile Homes

The taxation of mobile homes can vary greatly from state to state. In some states, they are treated more like vehicles than homes. In others, they are assessed and taxed like ordinary residences. The following applies to those states in which mobile homes are treated as real estate for property tax purposes.

Manufactured homes, as these units are now called, pose an especially difficult problem for both assessors and appeals boards. That's because it is difficult to compare the value of a unit in a highly desirable first-class mobile home park with the same unit on an unattractive lot surrounded by wrecked cars and tree stumps.

Assessors try to compile detailed sales statistics on mobile homes by size, brand and model year. And each year, assessors apply trending adjustments based on these sales. Assessors claim that mobile home values generally tend to follow single-family home sales, especially at times when the real estate market is hot.

This contention is rebutted by the claim of many mobile home owners that their residences should be valued more like automobiles than standard homes because they depreciate each year. And they point to the industry's value guide to show how the prices of models decline each year.

This depreciation argument is not sufficient to win an appeal because the sales statistics do not bear out the claim. In order to win an appeal, mobile home owners have to build a case based on the specifics of their property, as described in the previous chapter.

Experienced board members get a feel for mobile home values and tend to provide relief when an assessment takes a large jump in any one year. The condition of the mobile home can be a key factor in the board's decision, and photos showing dilapidation can be extremely helpful.

CASE STUDY: The Mobile Home Dilemma

Facts:

Ted Rosario owned a large mobile home situated on his own lot in the country. He paid $36,000 for the manufactured home about 18 months before receiving his assessment. The new valuation was for $42,500, an 18 percent increase over the previous year's new value. Rosario went to a mobile home dealer and was told he should appeal because manufactured homes depreciate like cars, that the "blue book" on his unit was $32,800 and that the $42,500 assessment was ridiculous. Rosario filed an appeal and told the board essentially what the dealer had told him. The assessor reported that the 18 percent increase was based on sales of *similar make and model mobile homes throughout the county during the previous year, when there was an especially hot real-estate market throughout the state.*

Decision:

Rosario won a reduction in his assessment to $39,000, an increase of about 8 percent from the previous year.

Reasoning:

Mobile home appeals present difficult issues for appeals boards because these units are not sold in an organized market like other homes. Upon consultation with the assessor's staff, the board learned that most mobile homes in the county had been increased about 8 percent but that Rosario's model happened to fall into a category with a sales record indicating that a much higher increase was warranted. It turned out that most of these models were located in high-end mobile home parks, not on rural lots like Rosario's. The board that year reduced numerous motor home assessments that exceeded 8 percent.

Apartments

The assessment of apartments and other business properties can follow a substantially different procedure from the valuation of homes and bare land. Often, there are not enough sales of business properties so that assessors can establish value based on market transactions. Secondly, property values in the business world are determined more from the income produced by a facility than from the intrinsic value of the land and buildings.

In some areas, there will be sufficient sales of apartment complexes so that assessment adjustments will be based, at least in part, on the open market. But often the assessor will employ the so-called income approach based on the actual and potential revenues and expenses from an apartment structure. Such factors as age, condition and vacancies may also be taken into consideration.

Because the valuation of apartments can be complicated, the assessor's office often goes through a procedure akin to negotiation with the property owner in order to arrive at a fair figure.

Appeals by apartment owners occasionally come before citizen boards, which ordinarily do not have the expertise to analyze complex presentations involving alternate methods of valuation. If a board feels that it does not have the tools to make a ruling, it has the option of sustaining the assessor's valuation and in essence pushing the property owner into a further appeal to the next appropriate authority, which can be a tax court or a state-level hearing.

Retail Stores

Commercial property likewise is usually appraised by the income approach. Owners of unsuccessful shopping centers and other retail space often appeal for relief. The argument is simple: So much of the space is vacant that the property's value on the open market is much reduced.

But the issues involved in appraisal of commercial property is anything but simple for the lay members of appeals boards. Many factors are usually taken into consideration in the appraisal of retail establishments, and each development poses a unique set of problems and circumstances.

The property owner has several shots at reductions: negotiations with the assessor, a petition before the appeals board, and further appeal to the state authorities or the courts. Few owners of commercial property get relief from citizen boards, unless it is recommended by the assessor's office, because boards are often instructed not to decide issues involving complex business properties but rather to send the matter on to supposed experts at a higher level of government.

Industrial Properties

The valuation of large factories and other high-value industrial property is considered so technical that states often do not allow local assessors to appraise them. That job goes to the state "experts" who forward the assessments each year to the county assessor. Small industrial properties are assessed locally. In most states, public utility property is assessed by a state agency rather than a local jurisdiction.

Owners of industrial property frequently hire experts to appraise their parcels and determine whether the assessments are reasonable. These independent appraisers, who specialize in industrial property, may provide the owner with the basis for an appeal. What usually follows is that the independent appraiser meets with the state or county assessors in an effort to reach an agreed value. Often, this results in the stipulation to a new assessed value, and the board is asked to ratify that figure (which it usually does).

If the two sides cannot agree, the property owner can try to make a case before the citizen board. But that is almost always doomed to failure because few board members have any special knowledge about industrial property. So these petitions usually go up the ladder to the state appeals authority. In some states, the hearing officer can face the unusual situation in which an appraiser from his or her own agency is defending an assessment.

Case Study: A Leak in the Underground

Facts:

The Excelsior Oil Company had a leaking gasoline tank in a service station and was ordered by environmental authorities to replace the tank and eliminate the underground contamination within six months. The property was assessed at $292,000, and the cost of *satisfying the government order was $80,000. The company requested an assessment reduction on the grounds that the value of the property had been reduced as a result of the contamination.*

Decision:

The board granted Excelsior a one-year reduction of $80,000.

Reasoning:

The board agreed with Excelsior that the market value of the service station had been reduced by the amount needed to eliminated the tank leakage problem. But the board also notified the assessor that this was a temporary reduction caused by a specific problem rather than by a change in the inherent value of the parcel. The following year, the assessment was raised $96,000 to reflect the $80,000, plus the trend factor for commercial properties in the area.

Farm and Timber Land

Some states grant owners of farm and timber land special reductions in assessments. These special rates, below what the acreage would bring on the open market, are established each year by the state. Ordinarily, the appeals process cannot be used to obtain a reduction in specially assessed land. (Anyone seeking to obtain specially assessed status for land should obtain the proper forms at the assessor's office.)

Personal Property

The taxation of personal property varies tremendously from state to state. Generally, property taxes are levied only on tools and equipment used for a trade or business. The usual practice is for each business to file lists of personal property with the assessor each year, and a state-set depreciation schedule is used to establish a value for each item. It is important to note that household furniture and other personal items are usually exempt from taxation. Furniture used in a business office, however, can be subject to assessment.

Many businesses fail to file up-to-date inventories of their personal property, and as a result they are often taxed on items that have been discarded. On the other hand, assessors do not visit every place of business every year to take inventory and make sure every item is reported. A good rule of thumb for businesses is to file the same lists for both income and property taxation.

Because the method of assessment is keyed to a state-developed depreciation schedule, it is difficult to win an appeal based on over-valuation by the assessor's office. But there are approaches that could be successful: Often worthless equipment remains on the premises and it is still assessed at 30 percent of purchase price. By demolishing the equipment or removing it, the property owner can present a valid argument for reduction. On occasion, an inaccurate list is filed with the assessor to the detriment of the property owner.

Ordinarily, personal property appeals are confidential, with the public excluded from the board room. This is partially because confidential income tax records of the appellant may be used in consideration of the appeal. Privacy is also designed to protect any trade secrets of the petitioner.

Personal property appeals ordinarily do not involve large sums of money because very expensive pieces of machinery affixed to a building are normally assessed as part of the structure.

5

A Winning Strategy

Many property owners decline to challenge their property-tax assessments simply because they are afraid to present their cases before panels of public officials. For some reason, they feel that the experience will be emotional, that they will make fools of themselves because they are not experts at presenting testimony, and that they will face board members who are insensitive government bureaucrats with a natural bias toward high assessments.

The facts: Board hearings are usually quite informal, far different from courtroom proceedings. Board members, in most jurisdictions, are ordinary citizens who have volunteered their time, and they serve as referees between the assessor and the taxpayers. These board members would rather receive folksy evidence from ordinary citizens than slick presentations from attorneys and real-estate professionals.

As Franklin Delano Roosevelt said as the nation entered World War II, "there is nothing to fear except fear itself." Any citizen who feels an assessment is too high ought to appeal. There is little to lose and a tax rebate to gain. Board members will be gentle, even helpful, to petitioners unless they try to present cases based on deception and lies.

Try to envision your appeal from the board's point of view.

First, keep in mind that boards often have heavy caseloads and operate under stringent time restrictions. A petitioner may be given as few as five 5 minutes to present an appeal, including questions from the members. However, 15 minutes is more typical, and small counties with relatively few appeals tend to be even more generous.

Second, try to answer the questions the board wants answered: "What is your property worth on the open market? Why is it worth less than the assessment? What is your proof?"

If you can't provide convincing answers to these questions, you are not ready to present an appeal.

Every appeal should be based on answers to these questions. The board action is based simply on a comparison between the assessment and the figure proposed by the petitioner — and the evidence each side presents. The assessor need not present evidence because the annual ratio report has already been approved, and the benefit of the doubt ordinarily goes to the assessor.

Many appellants try to base their cases on such factors as national and regional economic conditions, national and regional home sales, asking prices for current listings, the time properties remain on the market, alternate systems of appraisal and the like. Boards view this kind of evidence as essentially irrelevant, and it can hurt a case more than it can help it.

Boards want to hear facts about recent sales of comparable properties, the cost to cure any extraordinary problems with the subject property, details about assessment inequalities in the immediate neighborhood and other such evidence discussed in the previous chapter.

Heart of the Appeal

The attitude of the petitioner can play an important part in the appeals process. Boards want to hear a petitioner get right to the heart of the appeal, present the essence of the case verbally, back it up with the right supporting documents and then prepare to answer questions.

Board members are human beings. They don't want to be bored by presentation of irrelevant material. They don't want to be attacked as representatives of a tax-eating government monster or as adjuncts to the assessor's office. Nor do they want to hear about property tax burdens and how they are driving people out of their homes, although in rare instances hardship appeals can work for long-time owners of property that is barely habitable.

Here are answers to some commonly asked questions about assessment appeals:

Should I bring a map to the hearing?

The board probably will have a map of your neighborhood available, but there may be some benefit in bringing a map of your immediate area showing the location of your parcel and any comparable properties being used as the basis of the appeal.

Should I bring copies of my tax bill?

That would not be necessary because the basic information about your parcel and its assessment has previously been copied onto the petition which is before the board. Remember that the board is interested only in assessments and market values of property, not the property tax.

Should I bring pictures of the property?

Photos can be extremely helpful to show extraordinary depreciation such as water damage and foundation cracks. But don't bring so many pictures that you will diffuse the impact from the most dramatic shots. Also, it isn't a bad idea to bring one overview shot of the property just so the board can see what you are talking about. In some jurisdictions, the assessor's photo will be available to the board, but it could be 15 or 20 years old.

Should I hire an attorney or an appraiser to present my case?

Unless you have an extraordinarily complex appeal hanging on a legal issue or some fine point of appraisal, you are better off making the presentation yourself. Professionals usually appear only on appeals involving commercial and industrial properties with complicated assessment evaluations.

If I have a good case, why can't I just present it in writing?

You can. The risk is that you will lose because you have not provided the answer to a question the board considers vital. It is probably safer to make an appearance and bring every document with you that might be relevant. Even if you plan to appear, it is best to put your case on paper (one page if possible) and present it to the board. That way you will be sure you have made your points and you need not fear about getting the jitters. Then you can just make a brief statement and answer questions. The board simply wants to strip the case down to its fundamental issues and determine whether the assessment is reasonable or not. You should concentrate on helping the board get down to basics, and it doesn't make much difference whether this is done orally or in writing.

What documents do I need?

That depends on the grounds for the appeal. See the previous chapters for a guide to each type of appeal. The most common error is that taxpayers present a deed or closing statement from a title company showing the price paid for a parcel of property. To the taxpayer, that looks like sufficient evidence that a certain price was paid on a certain date and that the assessment should be adjusted accordingly. But the board wants to know whether there was a standard real estate commission paid, whether the property had been on the open market for a reasonable time, whether there was anything unusual in the sale, and what date the deal was struck. Much of that information can be provided by the earnest money contract signed by both parties at the time the house is sold but before the deal becomes final.

Where can I get up-to-date sales information?

That information can be obtained from several sources, usually at little or no cost. These sources include the county assessor's office, real estate brokers and title insurance companies. There are also firms providing listings of properties by street, with sales included, but the information on sales may not be up to date.

What do I do if I'm convinced the assessment is high but I don't know how high?

Board members also can get gut feelings that assessments are high, but they shouldn't grant reductions on that basis. The petitioner must put a dollar amount on the appeal form and must find some rationale to support it. If there have been recent sales of neighboring parcels, these should provide the best indicator of value. Far too many petitioners simply seek the previous year's assessment without giving any recognition to activity in the real estate market.

If I lose my first appeal, should I appeal further up the ladder?

That depends on the circumstances. If you learned from this experience and can now make a stronger case at the next level, by all means do so. Also, there is a subtle change in the burden of proof as an appeal moves up the ladder, with the assessor under more pressure to justify the valuation. In some states, assessors must defend their assessments in writing and must make a physical inspection of each parcel before the hearing. Sometimes boards deny appeals simply because they do not have adequate documentation or information, rather than because the cause was unjust.

6

Dos and Don'ts

In no particular order, here is a list of suggestions in a Do-and-Don't format that should help property owners decide whether they should appeal, how to prepare their evidence and how to present their cases to an appeals board.

Don't challenge the appraisal system required by the state and used by every local assessor.

Do take advantage of the fundamental flaw in that system and show how it results in an overassessment of your property.

Don't base your appeal on the rise in property taxes, the property tax burden or the trend of taxes over the year.

Do place the emphasis on the assessment and how it may differ from the value established by the real estate market in your neighborhood.

Don't be afraid to appeal and appear before a board or hearing officer. The board members are usually ordinary citizens like yourself and will listen to reason.

Do keep in mind that a large percentage of petitioners receive reductions, many of them recommended by the local assessor.

Don't base your appeal on comparisons based on square footage or acreage.

Do remember the general rule that the larger the building the lower the assessment per square foot. (The same guideline applies to acreage.)

Don't place any emphasis on the asking prices of properties or the sluggishness of the real-estate market in your area.

Do place the emphasis on actual sales of properties comparable to yours. Remember that the law requires that appraisers base their assessments on actual sales, regardless of how long the property was on the market and regardless of how many times the asking price was dropped.

Don't file a written appeal with skimpy information and expect the board to flush out the information.

Do complete every blank on the petition thoroughly. Submit whatever documents are advisable to substantiate your claims, and appear before the board to underscore your main points and answer any questions.

Don't overload the board with documents, maps, photographs, tax bills and written arguments.

Do try to envision the appeal from the board's viewpoint. Be as brief as possible and stick to the main points. Too much paper and too much palaver might lead the board to think it was getting a snow job.

Don't base an appeal on general economic conditions or the national or regional housing market, as evidenced by reports in the newspapers.

Do base the appeal on the specifics of the subject property and its immediate neighborhood.

Don't assume that an opinion from a local real estate agent — or even a licensed appraiser — will automatically produce a reduction.

Do keep in mind that boards are leery of information from these sources and will analyze their opinions thoroughly to see whether the properties selected by these sources are truly comparable to yours. Often appraisers will use parcels miles away from the subject as comps, and boards give these appraisals little weight.

Don't assume that you are an automatic winner because you recently purchased the property at a price below the assessed value.

Do provide proof that the sale was an arm's length transaction through a real estate broker and that the property had been on the market for a reasonable period of time. Also, keep in mind that the sales price is subject to time trending from the date the offer was made until the start of the tax year.

Don't try to win a reduction based on normal wear and tear on a building. Every building needs periodic painting, roof replacement and the like.

Do by all means base an appeal on an exceptional damage to the property. This is one of the best ways to win a reduction if the cost to cure is presented, especially if the damage is confirmed by an inspector from the assessor's office.

Don't try to conceal important information about the property. The assessor's records are often surprisingly complete, and a board will turn against you if you present inaccurate or deceptive information.

Do let representatives of the assessor's office into your property. You have a legal right not to let them inside your residence, but that will hurt you at the time of a board hearing. The best approach is to appear completely open, even if it may hurt.

Don't attack government in general, the assessor or the tax system. Letting off steam might make you feel better, but it won't help you get a tax rebate.

Do stick to the specific facts regarding the real market value of your property and the information you have gathered to support the figure you have presented to the board.

Don't act dumb in presenting your appeal and expect the board in effect to make your case for you.

Do understand that the board expects every petitioner to be familiar with the basics of the tax system and to present a reasonably informed appeal. However, that does not mean the appeal must be presented in a professional fashion, as might be done by an attorney, a professional appraiser or a tax consultant.

Don't assume you have an airtight case because you have a certified appraisal showing a lower value.

Do make sure there are no flaws in a certified appraisal, especially if it was prepared for refinancing, rather than for an initial mortgage loan.

Don't base your case on legal issues, such as disputes with government agencies. These issues can only be decided by courts, not by boards of equalization.

Do emphasize errors made by the assessor in setting a value for your property. Find some way to prove that your particular parcel is an exception to the value trends established for your community.

7

Summary

Here, in short form, are the steps that should be taken to optimize your chances of winning a reduction in your assessment and thus your property taxes.

Upon receiving your property tax bill, examine it closely and determine to the best of your ability whether the assessment seems too high.

Unless you are sure that the assessment reflects the real market value of your property (or less), start taking the steps necessary to see whether the assessment is too high. (It is important to note that some states use a percentage of market value as the basis for assessment.)

Remember that the assessment system is based on averages (called "trends") and some properties are always assessed too high. Among the steps that can be taken:

- Check the assessor's records to determine whether it contains any mistakes.

- Ask a real estate agent who specializes in your neighborhood what your property would bring on the open market.

- Obtain an updated listing of sales in your area and see whether your assessment tracks with the market for comparable properties.

If you now believe that the assessment is high, develop the specific grounds for the appeal. (See chapter 3.) Develop the evidence needed to make a convincing case. Try to use one or two grounds. Don't try a smorgasbord approach hoping by chance that you will hit upon a tidbit the board will find tasty.

Get an appeal petition from the clerk of the appeals board. (These forms may also be available from the assessor's office.).

Fill out the form carefully and completely. Provide the basic evidence for your case. What you write on the form may be more important than what you say at the hearing.

Make sure you mail the form by the deadline.

If you are absolutely certain you have made the best possible case on paper, a decision not to appear at the hearing will not be held against you. But it is usually best to appear so you can answer any questions the board may ask or provide documents you may have neglected to submit.

What should you do if you discover at the hearing that the assessor has recommended a reduction, but not for the full amount you requested? As a general rule, take what the assessor has offered if the board seems willing to grant it. By fighting for more, you risk losing what the assessor has recommended and you will be working against the odds trying to get more.

If the board declines to give you a reduction and you are still convinced you are right, should you go further up the appeals ladder? That depends on the validity of the case. There may be advantages to a state-level hearing. For example, you have more time to obtain evidence and perfect your case, and the state may insist that the assessor inspect the property before the hearing.

Even if you can't make a good case for an appeal this year, keep in mind that you may have a better chance next year. If you keep an eye on the real estate market in your community, if only through newspaper ads, you'll be able to recognize an assessment that may be too high.

Try to identify homes in your neighborhood that are comparable to yours in every important way — quality, size, lot size, extras. When one is sold, find out the purchase price and compare it to your assessment. That's the best way to keep track of the value of your parcel. And if it falls below the assessment, you'll know it's probably time to file an appeal.

If you follow these steps, there's a fair chance that one of these days you'll be the proud recipient of a property-tax rebate check.

For Further Assistance...

This book spells out the basic principles of assessment appeals. Because there are so many variances from state to state, it is impossible to provide hard-and-fast rules that will apply in all situations. Chapter 8 will provide a summary of the appeals procedures in each state but does not detail the idiosyncrasies of each taxing jurisdiction.

If you have questions about the process in your community, you can usually get straight answers from your local assessor, from state property-tax administrators or from clerks of local appeals boards. If your problems involve complex legal or appraisal issues, it might be advisable to consult with at attorney specializing in property-tax matters, with a licensed appraiser or with a property-tax consultant. However, be forewarned that the cost of hiring one of these experts could exceed the potential savings from a tax reduction.

Part II
STATE
GUIDELINES

8

State Appeals Systems

Every state in the union has a property tax in one form or another, and there is surprising uniformity in the way the assessment and appeals systems operate. Assessments are established in most states by county, but city and township valuations are common in the northeast. Maryland and Montana operate statewide assessment systems.

Appeal procedures vary primarily in details, while the basic system is fairly uniform. The first step is often an informal meeting with the assessor in an attempt at reconciliation, followed by an appeal to a county or local board.

Taxpayers generally can take their appeals into the court system, but these protests are normally worthwhile only if the appeal centers on a legal (rather than a valuation) issue or there is a very large amount of money involved.

Most states have central agencies that administer the assessment laws, that equalize property taxation between counties and that on occasion provide an avenue for appeals. The following state-by-state listings are designed for ordinary citizens appealing their land and home values rather than for large corporations with complex industrial properties. The list provides the assessment jurisdiction, an outline of the appeals procedure, and an address and phone number of a state or local agency which can provide additional information.

ALABAMA

Assessing jurisdiction: County.

Appeals process: Citizens are given a deadline for filing appeals with the county Board of Equalization after receipt of notice of increase or publication of the assessment roll. Dates will vary from county to county, but the deadline is normally 10 days after the notice is mailed or published. Boards of Equalization usually sit in June and July. Decisions can be appealed further to the county Circuit Court and thereafter all the way to the state Supreme Court.

For further information contact:

State Department of Revenue
50 N. Ripley St.
Montgomery AL 36132-7210
(205) 242-1525

ALASKA

Taxing jurisdiction: Municipality or borough. (Note: Some remote parts of Alaska have no local governments, no services or taxes.)

Appeals process: Each local Board of Equalization sets its own appeals period. Typically, a taxpayer would have 30 days following the issuance of an assessment notice to file an appeal. A board decision may be appealed to the state Superior Court.

For further information contact:

State Department of Revenue
550 W. 7th Ave.
Anchorage, AK 99501
(907) 276-1363

ARIZONA

Assessing jurisdiction: County.

Appeals process: Assessors normally mail value notices after Nov. 15, and taxpayers are given at least 30 days thereafter to file an appeal with the assessor. Citizens may appeal further to the county Board of Equalization within 10 days after receiving a ruling from the assessor. The next step is the state Board of Tax Appeals. This process can be circumvented, especially when the appeal is based on a legal rather than a valuation issue, by a direct appeal to the state Superior Court.

For further information contact:

State Department of Revenue
1600 W. Monroe St., Suite 801
Phoenix, AZ 85038
(602) 542-5221

ARKANSAS

Assessing jurisdiction: County.

Appeals process: There are a series of deadlines in August, September and October. The first protest goes to the county Board of Equalization, thereafter to the County Court and Circuit Court. The process depends on what the Board of Equalization does with the assessment.

For further information contact:

Public Service Commission
1614 W. 3rd St.
Little Rock, AK 72201
(501) 324-9240

CALIFORNIA

Assessing jurisdiction: County.

Appeals process: Taxpayers first should try to win reductions through informal protests to assessors. (Remember that California has an unusual system. The assessment is based on the purchase price, with increases limited to 2 percent a year.) The formal process begins with an appeal, which ordinarily must be filed between July 2 and Sept. 15, with the county Board of Equalization (Board of Supervisors) or Board of Assessment Appeals. Further appeals, consisting of a review of the record, can be made to the Superior Court.

For further information contact:

State Board of Equalization
1719 24th St.
Sacramento, CA 95816
(916) 445-4982

COLORADO

Assessing jurisdiction: County.

Appeals process: Taxpayers file protests with the county assessor during the month of May. The assessor must complete the decision-making process by the end of June, and citizens may appeal by July 15 with the county Board of Equalization, which may be composed of the county commissioners. Thereafter, appeals may be taken to the State Board of Assessment Appeals or the District Court. Cases can go all the way to the Supreme Court. (The timetable for protesting personal property assessments is slightly different.)

For further information contact:

Division of Property Taxation
1313 Sherman St.
Denver, CO 80203
(303) 866-2371

CONNECTICUT

Assessing jurisdiction: Municipality.

Appeals process: The first step is an informal meeting with the assessor. That is followed with an appeal before the local Board of Review, which meets during the month of February. Appointments can be made through the assessor's office or by appearing at a board meeting in February. The procedure is informal and varies some-what from community to community. Further appeals can be made to the Superior Court.

For further information contact:

Office of Policy and Management
80 Washington St.
Hartford, CT 06106
(203) 566-8170.

DELAWARE

Assessing jurisdiction: County.

Appeals process: Appeals procedures vary from county to county. In New Castle County (Wilmington area), March 15 is the deadline for filing with the Board of Appeals. An informal conference with the assessor can be sought prior to that date. Protests can eventually be taken to the county Superior Court.

For further information contact:

Assessor's Office
New Castle County
800 French St.
Wilmington, DE 19801
(302) 571-7637

There is no statewide assessment coordinating agency in Delaware.

DISTRICT OF COLUMBIA

Assessing jurisdiction: City (district).

Appeals process: Appeals must be filed by April 15 with the District Board of Equalization and Review. Thereafter, appeals may be taken to the tax court division of the Superior Court and eventually to the district Supreme Court.

For further information contact:

Board of Equalization
300 Indiana Ave. NW, Room 5126
Washington, DC 20001
(202) 727-6460

FLORIDA

Assessing jurisdiction: County.

Appeals process: Following receipt of an assessment, the first step is an informal conference with the assessor. The deadline for filing with the county Value Adjustment Board is the 25th day after the assessor mails the notice of value. Further appeals can be made to the county Circuit Court, then to the state Supreme Court.

For further information contact:

Department of Revenue
5050 W. Tennessee St.
Tallahassee, FL 32399-0100
(904) 488-0108

GEORGIA

Assessing jurisdiction: County.

Appeals process: Taxpayers may file appeals with the county Board of Tax Assessors within 30 days after receiving the assessment notice. If the Board makes no change in the assessment, the appeal is automatically forwarded to the county Board of Equalization for hearing. (If a change is made, the taxpayer has 21 days to decide whether to pursue further appeals.) Citizens may eventually take their appeals to the Superior Court, Court of Appeals and state Supreme Court.

For further information, contact:

Department of Revenue
405 Trinity-Washington Bldg.
Atlanta, GA 30334
(404) 656-4240

HAWAII

Assessing jurisdiction: County.

Appeals process: Citizens may seek informal conferences with the assessor. The deadline for formal appeals is April 9, and taxpayers may file by that date either with the county Board of Review or with the Tax Appeals Court. Eventually, appeals may be taken to the state Supreme Court.

For further information contact:

Property Assessment Division
842 Bethel St.
Honolulu, HI 96813
(808) 527-5500

IDAHO

Assessing jurisdiction: County.

Appeals process: The first step is an informal conference with the assessor. If that fails, the taxpayer has until the fourth Monday in June to file with the county Board of Equalization. Ordinarily, citizens have a month following receipt of a notice from the Board of Equalization to petition the State Board of Tax Appeals. Finally, appeals may be filed with the District Court and the state Supreme Court.

For further information contact:

Department of Revenue and Taxation
700 W. State St. (P.O. Box 36)
Boise, ID 83722
(208) 334-7733

ILLINOIS

Assessing jurisdiction: Township, with one major exception, Cook County (Chicago).

Appeals process: Every assessment notice contains a deadline for appeal with the local Board of Review. August 31 is a common deadline. Appeals can then be taken to the state Property Tax Appeals Board, and thereafter to the Circuit and Superior Courts. In Cook County, appeals should first be taken to the assessor, then to the Board of Appeals. Filing deadlines may vary within the county, depending on the date of assessment notice.

For further information contact:

Property Tax Appeals Board
404 Stratton Office Bldg.
Springfield, IL 62706-0002
(217) 782-6076

INDIANA

Assessing jurisdiction: Township.

Appeals process: Appeals must be filed with the county Board of Review within 30 days of the mailing date on the assessment notice from the assessor. If the citizen is not satisfied with the action of the county board, the appeal can be taken to the state Board of Tax Commissioners within 30 days after the ruling is issued by the local board. The Indiana Tax Court is the third tier in the appeal process.

For further information contact:

Board of Tax Commissioners
201 State Office Bldg.
Indianapolis, IN 46204
(317) 232-3761

IOWA

Assessing jurisdiction: Mostly counties, some cities.

Appeals process: Appeals must be filed with the local Board of Review by May 5. Further appeals may be taken to the county District Court and the state Supreme Court.

For further information contact:

Department of Revenue and Finance
Hoover State Office Bldg.
Des Moines, IA 50319
(515) 281-4040

KANSAS

Assessing jurisdiction: County.

Appeals process: Taxpayers first appeal to the county appraiser, with the deadline 21 days after the assessment notice is mailed. The appraiser normally conducts informal hearings in March and hands down decisions in early April. The next avenue of appeal is a county hearing officer appointed by the county commissioners. The third level of appeal is the state Board of Tax Appeals, followed by the District Court and finally the state Supreme Court.

For further information contact:

Division of Property Valuation
Docking State Office Bldg.
Topeka, KS 66612-1585
(913) 296-2365

KENTUCKY

Taxing jurisdiction: County, except for city of Fort Thomas.

Appeals process: Property owners must first appeal in writing or by telephone with the local property valuation administrator. This must be done in the 13 days following the fourth Monday in May (not including Sundays). The next step is the county Board of Assessment Appeals, and protests must be filed by the 14th day after the fourth Monday in May. Thereafter, appeals may be taken to the Kentucky Board of Tax Appeals and the Circuit Court.

For further information contact:

Department of Property Taxation
592 E. Main St.
Frankfort, KY 40620
(502) 564-6730

LOUISIANA

Assessing jurisdiction: Parish (county).

Appeals process: The first step is an informal conference with the assessor in August or September. The next step is the filing of a formal appeal with the Board of Review, and the deadline varies from parish to parish. Further appeals can be made with the state Tax Commission or the District Court.

For further information contact:

Tax Commission
5420 Corporate Blvd.
Baton Rouge, LA 70808
(504) 925-7830

MAINE

Assessing jurisdictions: Cities, towns, unincorporated townships.

Appeals process: Taxpayers have six months after receipt of an assessment notice to file an appeal with the local assessor, who has 60 days to respond. If the appeal is denied, the citizen may file with the local Board of Assessment Review or the County Commissioners. The Superior Court provides a third level of appeal.

For further information contact:

State Tax Assessor
State House
Augusta, ME 04333
(207) 289-2011

MARYLAND

Assessing jurisdiction: State, which has assessment offices in every county and the city of Baltimore.

Appeals process: Within 45 days after an assessment notice is mailed, taxpayers may file appeals with the State Department of Assessment. If denied, the appeal may be channeled to the Property Tax Assessment Appeals Board and then to the Maryland Tax Court, the Circuit Court and the Court of Special Appeals.

For further information, contact:

Department of Assessment
301 W. Preston St.
Baltimore, MD 21201
(301) 225-1191

MASSACHUSETTS

Assessing jurisdictions: Cities and towns.

Appeals process: Protests are taken initially to the local assessing authority. The deadline is Oct. 1 or 30 days after the mailing of the notice of assessment, whichever is later. Thereafter, the appeal may be taken to the County Commissioners, the Appellate Tax Court and eventually to the Appeals Court and the state Supreme Judicial Court.

For further information contact:

Division of Local Services
100 Cambridge St.
Boston, MA 02114-9655
(617) 727-2300

MICHIGAN

Assessing jurisdictions: Cities and townships.

Appeals process: Citizens first must appear before the local Board of Review at a time specified by the city or town authorities. This is done in March in most communities. The next step is a written appeal to the State Tax Tribunal, with a deadline of June 30. The last step is the state court system.

For further information contact:

State Tax Tribunal
1033 S. Washington Ave.
(P.O. Box 30302)
Lansing, MI 48909
(517) 334-6521

MINNESOTA

Assessing jurisdictions: Township, city and county.

Appeals process: Taxpayers have two avenues of appeal. One is a direct filing with the state Tax Court, and the deadline for filing is May 15 of the year the property tax is due. The more informal process starts with an informal conference with the local assessor in April or May. The filing procedure varies from jurisdiction to jurisdiction. The next step is an appearance before the county Board of Equalization, which meets the first day of the last 10 working days in June and may remain in session for as long as two weeks. The final step is an appeal to the small claims or regular division of the Tax Court, depending on the amount of the assessment.

For further information contact:

Local Government Services
Mail Station 3340
St. Paul, MN 55146-3340
(612) 296-2286

MISSISSIPPI

Assessing jurisdiction: County.

Appeals process: An informal meeting with the local assessor is the first step, followed by a hearing before the county Board of Supervisors. Appeals must be filed with the board by the first Monday in July, and hearings are normally conducted in August. Further appeals may be taken to the Circuit Court and eventually the state Supreme Court.

For further information contact:

State Tax Commission
Woolfolk Bldg. (P.O. Box 1033)
Jackson, MS 39205-0960
(601) 359-1076

MISSOURI

Assessing jurisdiction: County.

Appeals process: Appeals are first taken to the county Board of Equalization, and filing deadlines vary from county to county. The second step is the filing of an appeal with the state Tax Commission. For large counties, the deadline is August 15 or 30 days from receipt of a notice from the Board of Equalization, For all other counties, the deadline is Sept. 30. The county Circuit Court is the third level of appeal.

For further information contact:

Tax Commission
621 E. Capitol Ave.
Jefferson City, MO 65102-0146
(314) 751-2414

MONTANA

Assessing jurisdiction: Montana has a hybrid system in which the assessment system is controlled by the state, but most assessors are elected by county.

Appeals process: Appeals are first filed with the county Tax Appeals Board. The deadline is the first Monday in June or 15 days following receipt of the assessment notice, whichever is later. Thereafter, appeals may be taken to the state Tax Appeals Board and the District Court. Citizens have 30 days to file with the state board after receiving a notice from the local board, and 60 days to file with the court after receiving notice from the state board.

For further information contact:

Department of Revenue
616 Helena Ave.
Helena, MT 59620
(406) 443-0811

NEBRASKA

Assessing jurisdiction: County.

Appeals procedure: An informal meeting with the county assessor is recommended, preferably between Jan. 1 and April 1. Formal appeals may be filed with the county clerk for a hearing by the Board of Equalization within 30 days after the assessor publishes a notice of completion of the assessment roll. The county boards meet between April 1 and May 30. Appeals may eventually be taken to the District Court.

For further information contact:

Department of Revenue
P.O. Box 94818
Lincoln, NE 68509
(402) 471-2971

NEVADA

Assessing jurisdiction: County

Appeals process: Appeals must be filed with the county Board of Equalization by Jan. 15. The next appeal goes to the state Board of Equalization, which has a deadline of the first Monday in March. Appeals may also be taken to the county District Court.

For further information contact:

Division of Assessment Standards
Capitol Complex
Carson City, NV 89710
(702) 687-4840

NEW HAMPSHIRE

Assessing jurisdictions: Cities and townships.

Appeals process: Appeals should be filed with the local Board of Selectmen or other designated officials within two months after issuance of the tax bill. The next step is the New Hampshire Board of Tax and Land Appeals or with the Superior Court. The filing deadline is normally eight months after issuance of the tax bill.

For further information contact:

Department of Revenue Administration
61 S. Spring St. (P.O. Box 457)
Concord, NH 03302-0457
(603) 271-2687

NEW JERSEY

Assessing jurisdictions: City and township.

Appeals process: An informal meeting with the local assessor is the usual first step. A formal appeal may be filed with the county Board of Taxation by April 1. Within 45 days of a ruling by the board, a further appeal may be made with the state Tax Court. That court's decision can be appealed to the Superior Court.

For further information contact:

Division of Taxation
50 Barrack St.
Trenton, NJ 08646
(609) 292-7974

NEW MEXICO

Assessing jurisdiction: County.

Appeals process: The first step is the filing of an appeal with the county assessor within 30 days after the mailing of the valuation notice. Depending on the actions taken by the assessor, appeals may later be taken to a county Valuation Protest Board and the state Court of Appeals.

For further information contact:

Taxation and Revenue Department
P.O. Box 25162
Santa Fe, NM 87504
(505) 827-0700

NEW YORK

Assessing jurisdictions: Cities and townships.

Appeals process: Taxpayers are free to seek informal meetings with the assessor (tax commissioner in New York City) at any time before the tax roll is issued. Formal appeals are brought before the local Board of Assessment Review, which normally goes into session the fourth Tuesday in May. (This may vary in some communities.) Requests to be heard should be filed between May 1 and four business days prior to the fourth Tuesday in May. Further appeals may be taken to the state Supreme Court or small-claims court, depending on the amount of money involved.

For further information contact:

Div. of Equalization and Assessment
16 Sheridan Ave.
Albany, NY 12210-2714
(518) 474-8821

NORTH CAROLINA

Assessing jurisdiction: County.

Appeals process: An informal meeting with the assessor is the recommended first step. That is followed by a formal appeal before the county Board of Equalization and Review, which may consist of the county commissioners. The filing deadline is published every year and may vary somewhat from county to county. Generally, appeals may be filed between the first Monday in April and the first Monday in May, but the deadline is usually later in areas where physical reappraisals have been conducted. The next level of appeal is the state Property Tax Commission, and the filing deadline is 30 days following the mailing date of the notice from the county board. Finally, appeals may be taken to the Court of Appeals and the state Supreme Court.

For further information contact:

Department of Revenue
707 Hillsborough St., Suite 200
Williams-Cross Bldg.
Raleigh, NC 27603
(919) 733-7711

NORTH DAKOTA

Assessing jurisdictions: Cities and townships.

Appeals process: North Dakota has two avenues of appeal. The first is the informal process that can lead to hearings before the local, county and state boards of equalization. Every assessment notice includes the date when the local board will be in session, and citizens may present their protests at that time. The formal process starts with the filing of an application for abatement with the county auditor. Normally, this can be done within two years after an assessment is increased. This procedure starts with a local hearing, and the protest eventually can be considered by the district and supreme courts.

For further information contact:

Property Tax Division
State Capitol
Bismarck, ND 58505
(701) 224-3127

OHIO

Assessing jurisdiction: County.

Appeals process: By March 31 in the year following an assessment, an appeal must be filed with the county auditor to obtain a hearing before the County Board of Revision. Thereafter, the taxpayer has a choice of appealing to the state Board of Tax Appeals or the Court of Common Pleas. The deadline is 30 days after the mailing of a notice from the Board of Revision. Appeals may eventually be taken to the District Court of Appeals and the state Supreme Court.

For further information contact:

Department of Taxation
State Office Tower
Columbus, OH 43266-0030
(614) 466-5744

OKLAHOMA

Assessing jurisdiction: County.

Appeals process: Within 20 days of receiving a valuation notice, a taxpayer has 20 days to file for an informal meeting with the assessor. Petition forms are usually obtained from the county clerk. The first formal appeal can be filed with the county Board of Equalization within 15 days after the assessor makes a decision. Thereafter, the appeals process goes to the state Board of Property Tax Review to the District Court to the Supreme Court.

For further information contact:

State Tax Commission
2501 N. Lincoln Blvd.
Oklahoma City, OK 73194
(405) 521-3178

OREGON

Assessing jurisdiction: County.

Appeals process: Appeals must be filed with the county Board of Equalization by Dec. 31. Thereafter, appeals may be taken to the state Department of Revenue, the Oregon Tax Court and the state Supreme Court. Appeals based on specified narrow grounds may also be filed in June with each county's Board of Ratio Review.

For further information contact:

Department of Revenue
955 Center St. N.E.
Salem, OR 97310
(503) 378-3022

PENNSYLVANIA

Assessing jurisdiction: County. (Some counties are subdivided into assessment districts.)

Appeals process: The first step is an informal hearing with the assessor. Thereafter, appeals may be brought before a local Board of Revision of Taxes or a Board of Assessment Appeals. Filing deadlines, hearing dates and board procedures vary from area to area. Eventually, appeals may be taken to the Court of Common Pleas, the Superior Court and the state Supreme Court. Pennsylvania has perhaps the most complex appeals system in the nation, and taxpayers are advised to check the appeals process carefully in each county.

For further information contact: Local assessors. The Commonwealth of Pennsylvania performs no statewide coordinating or equalizing function, and there is no state agency charged with overseeing local assessment practices.

RHODE ISLAND

Assessing jurisdictions: Cities and townships.

Appeals process: The appeals process varies somewhat from community to community, depending on whether the city or township has an assessor or a part-time board of assessors. Generally, a protest must be filed with the local assessing authority within three months after the final day the property tax payment is due without penalty. In some communities, the second appeal is to a

Board of Assessment Review. Throughout the state, appeals may eventually be taken to the Superior Court.

For further information contact:

Office of Municipal Affairs
1 Capitol Hill
Providence, RI 02908-5873
(401) 277-6446

SOUTH CAROLINA

Assessing jurisdiction: County.

Appeals process: Initial appeals must be filed with the local assessor within 30 days of the mailing of a valuation notice. The next appeal may be taken to the county Board of Equalization within 10 days after the assessor makes a ruling. The final appeal on a valuation issue goes to the State Tax Commission. Legal questions may be taken to the court system.

For further information contact:

Tax Commission
301 Gervais St.
Columbia, SC 29214
(803) 737-4485

SOUTH DAKOTA

Assessing jurisdiction: County.

Appeals process: The first level of appeal is the city or township Board of Equalization, which convenes on the third Monday of April. Taxpayers need not make an appointment to be heard. But they must make an appointment with the county auditor to be heard by the county Board of Equalization, which begins hearings the second Tuesday in May. Further appeals may be taken to the state Board of Equalization and the Circuit Court.

For further information contact

Department of Revenue
700 Governor's Drive
Pierre, SD 57501-2276
(605) 773-3311

TENNESSEE

Assessing jurisdiction: County.

Appeals process: County boards of equalization go into session on June 1, and appointments are normally arranged through the assessor's office prior to that date. In some counties, protests may be brought by citizens walking into the hearing room. The state Board of Equalization provides the next level of appeal, with the deadline Aug. 1 or 45 days after the local board renders a decision, whichever is later. Legal issues may be brought before the Circuit Court.

For further information contact:

State Board of Equalization
505 Beaderick St., Suite 1600
Nashville, TN 37243
(615) 741-4883

TEXAS

Assessing jurisdictions: Counties and multi-county appraisal districts.

Appeals process: Taxpayers must file with the county Appraisal Review Board by June 1 or within 30 days of receipt of a valuation notice, whichever is later. Within 45 days after the board renders a decision, an appeal may be taken to the county District Court.

For further information contact:

Property Tax Division
4301 W. Bank Dr., Suite 150
Austin, TX 78746
(512) 329-7901

UTAH

Assessing jurisdiction: County.

Appeals process: A hearing before the local assessor is required before a formal appeal can be made. The deadline for filing with the county Board of Equalization varies from county to county, with Aug. 31 the date in the Salt Lake City area. Appeals may also be taken to the State Tax Commission and the State District Court.

For further information contact:

State Tax Commission
160 E. 300 S.
Salt Lake City, UT 84134
(801) 530-6297

VERMONT

Assessing jurisdictions: Cities and townships.

Appeals process: Within 14 days following the completion of the tax roll, appeals may be filed with the local Board of Listers or Board of Assessors. Dates vary from community to community. The next level of appeal is the local Board of Civil Authority, and taxpayers must file within 14 days after the decision by the Board of Listers. Finally, appeals may be taken to the state Director of Property Valuation or the Superior Court, and the deadline is 21 days from a ruling by the Board of Civil Authority.

For further information contact:

Division of Property Valuation
43 Randall St.
Waterbury, VT 05676
(802) 241-3500

VIRGINIA

Assessing jurisdictions: Cities and counties.

Appeals process: The first step is an informal appeal with the local assessor or board of assessors. Formal hearings are conducted by local boards of equalization, which meet at various times during the year. Some are in session all year long. Meeting dates are published or can be obtained by calling the local assessor's office. The Circuit Court provides the final level of appeal.

For further information contact:

Department of Taxation
2220 W. Broad St.
Richmond, VA 23201-2460
(804) 367-8020

WASHINGTON

Assessing jurisdiction: County.

Appeals process: The deadline for filing with the county Board of Equalization is July 15. Thereafter, appeals may be taken to the State Board of Tax Appeals and the Superior Court. Under some circumstances, the first step in the appeals process may be omitted and a protest may go directly to the state board. These appeals usually involve large and complicated business properties.

For further information contact:

Department of Revenue
6004 Capitol Blvd.
Tumwater, WA 98504
(206) 753-2057

WEST VIRGINIA

Assessing jurisdiction: County.

Appeals process: Appeals must be filed with the County Commissioner no later than Feb. 1, and hearings normally are conducted during February. The precise dates are published in local newspapers. Within 30 days after the local decision is rendered, the appeal may be taken to the Circuit Court. If the protest involves at least $50,000 or a constitutional issue, the appeal may be taken to the state Supreme Court of Appeal.

For further information contact:

State Tax Department
P.O. Box 2389
Charleston, WV 25328-2389
(304) 558-3333

WISCONSIN

Assessing jurisdictions: Cities, townships and villages.

Appeals process: The first step is an informal meeting with the assessor. A formal appeal may be brought before the local Board of Review, which begins hearings the second Monday in May. A request to be heard may be filed any time prior to adjournment of the board. In Milwaukee, the process starts with an appeal with the city tax commissioner, with a deadline of the third Monday in April. Further appeals can be filed with the state Department of Revenue or the Circuit Court.

For further information contact:

Department of Revenue
125 S. Webster St.
(P.O.Box 8933)
Madison, WI 53708
(608) 266-8661

WYOMING

Assessing jurisdiction: County.

Appeals process: Taxpayers are first urged to try to resolve any differences through an informal conference with the assessor. Formal appeals must be filed with the county Board of Equalization within 15 days after receipt of the valuation notice. Further appeals may be made to the state Board of Equalization and the county District Court.

For further information contact:

Department of Revenue and Taxation
122 W. 25th St.
Cheyenne, WY 82002
(307) 777-7215

Part III
GLOSSARY

GLOSSARY

The following definitions apply to the property-tax assessment and appeals systems. They may differ somewhat from standard dictionary definitions.

Before starting the alphabetized list of definitions, it is probably appropriate to comment about the term "real market value" listed in this glossary. Across the nation, there are numerous terms — among them *true market value, fair market value, full cash value* and *actual value* — used to describe what properties would bring on an open market. Legal definitions vary from state to state, and some states also base their assessments on a percentage of this market valuation. However, most taxpayers need not familiarize themselves with these technicalities in preparing their appeals because the key element is universal — open-market value.

Adverse location or environment — property so situated that its value is reduced by its proximity to an undesirable natural or man-made condition .

Appraisal — the valuation of a parcel of property, whether done by a government official or a private party.

Appellant — a property owner or other party petitioning for a reduction in an assessment.

Array — a term used by assessors to describe the list of properties of a certain category sold within a neighborhood within a given period of time, usually a year.

Assessor — the government official who establishes values for all properties within a jurisdiction for property-tax purposes.

Assessment — the valuation placed on a parcel by the assessor.

Buildability — the feasibility of constructing a home or other building on a piece of land. If an owner cannot obtain a building permit, the parcel may be considered "unbuildable."

Classification — the rating of homes by the assessor according to architectural features, construction quality and the like.

Comparable parcels or "comps" — properties similar to the subject parcel used by appraisers as a key element in establishing value.

Cost to cure — how much money would be required to repair damages to a building.

Deed — the formal document transferring property from one party to another.

Deferred maintenance — delayed normal repairs and upkeep to a property. This does not include extraordinary damages.

Earnest-money agreement — the contract signed by the buyer and seller during the offer-and -acceptance stage of negotiations for a piece of property.

Equalization — the term generally used to describe boards charged with hearing assessment appeals. It indicates that a prime task of the board is to equalize the tax burden among citizens with comparable properties.

Exceptional depreciation — exceptional damages to a building that are not the result of normal wear and tear.

Fee appraisal — a property valuation conducted by a licensed appraiser for a fee. These are most commonly ordered by financial institutions to determine value for mortgage purposes.

Improvements — a term commonly used by assessors to describe buildings. It refers to improvements to a piece of bare land, not to improvements on a building that had previously been built.

Inspection — the physical evaluation of a parcel by an assessor or appraiser.

Inspector — a representative of the assessor's office who conducts inspections.

Marketability — the feasibility of selling a parcel on the open market.

Mean, arithmetic and weighted — two measures used by assessors to determine how properties have increased or decreased in value during a tax year. These calculations are applied to the numbers obtained from a sales array.

Median — the middle parcel in a sales array arranged in ascending order of the sales price relative to the assessed value. If there are nine parcels, the fifth sale on the list would be the median.

Outbuildings — any barns, shops, sheds or other structures located on a lot in addition to a house or other main building.

Parcel — any piece of property that can be sold as a unit or listed on the tax rolls.

Personal property — equipment and tools used in a trade, business or factory. It normally does not apply to household goods, but assessment practices on personal property varies from state to state.

Petitioner — the property owner or other party appealing an assessment.

Ratio — the number used by the assessor to determine whether property in a neighborhood should be increased or decreased following analysis of sales trends.

Real market value — how much a parcel would bring on the open market.

Real property — land and buildings, as opposed to personal property consisting of tools and equipment.

Red flag — the designation often given a piece of property that is undergoing change and should be reevaluated every year until the project is completed.

Specially assessed value — a lower-than-market value placed on parcels as a matter of public policy. Special values are often placed on timber and farm land to prevent their conversion to urban usage.

Square footage — the floor space of a building. Assessors normally compute square footage from the outside of a structure, rounding off to the nearest foot. These figures will vary somewhat from price inside measurements of a building.

Trending — the process of determining true market value by using recent sales figures for each neighborhood and then applying an arithmetic increase or decrease factor to all properties within that neighborhood.

Trend factor — the number obtained for a neighborhood through the trending or ratio process.

Underimprovement — a structure on a piece of land that actually detracts from the value of the parcel as a whole. In these instances, it is appropriate to subtract the cost of removing the underimprovement from the true market value of the property because presumably that cost would have to be considered in the computation of the sales price of the parcel.

Part IV
APPENDIX

SAMPLE TAX BILL

	Code Area	Account Number
	007021	324580

Oregon Property Tax Year
JULY 1, 1992 TO JUNE 30, 1993

County **CLACKAMAS** **REAL**

Property Description (Map Number)

Township	Range	Section	1/4	1/16	Tax Lot	Special Interest
2S	1E	17	B	D	00200	

Acres	Property Class	Pull Number
	101	88-35596

Name & Address of Property Owner

Property Location

SEE INSERT FOR APPEAL RIGHTS
AND PAYMENT INSTRUCTIONS

See Taxing Detail on back of statement
for Breakdown of Taxes By District

PLEASE MAKE PAYMENT TO:

CLACKAMAS COUNTY TAX COLLECTOR
168 WARNER-MILNE ROAD
OREGON CITY, OR. 97045
(503)655-8671

VALUE CHANGE NOTICE

Real Market Value (RMV)	Last Year	This Year
RMV LAND	48,430	51,330
RMV BLDG	101,880	103,910
TOTAL RMV	150,310	155,240
NET ASSESSED VALUE	150,310	155,240

Property Taxes	3,491.79	3,397.59

PROPERTY TAX PAYMENT OPTIONS
(See insert for instructions and your appeal rights)

Pay	By	Discount Allowed		Net Amount
In Full	NOV 15	101.93	3%	3,295.66
2/3	NOV 15	45.30	2%	2,219.76
1/3	NOV 15	NONE		1,132.53

DELINQUENT TAXES

	Tax Year	Amount
Interest included through:		
11-15-92	Total Delinquent Amount	

Real property accounts with an unpaid balance for any tax year marked with an asterisk (') are subject to foreclosure if not paid on or before May 15. Any payments received on this account MUST be applied to delinquent taxes first.

TOTAL TAXES OWED ON THIS ACCOUNT IF PAID BY NOVEMBER 15	3,295.66

SAMPLE APPEAL FORM

REAL PROPERTY AND MOBILE HOME PETITION
TO THE BOARD OF EQUALIZATION OF _____ COUNTY, OREGON
(county where property is located)

I, _____ , request the board of equalization:
(owner of property or person in whose name the property is assessed)

☐ Reduce the real market or assessed value of the property described below for the 19 ____ – ____ tax year as provided in ORS 309.026.

☐ Excuse the 19 ____ – ____ Real Property Return late filing penalty of $ _____ imposed under ORS 308.295.

PROPERTY DESCRIPTION

Assessor's Account Number (from your tax statement)	Map and Tax Lot Number (from your tax statement)

Street Address of Property Being Appealed (if applicable)	Mobile Home: make, model, and "X" number

VALUE OF REAL PROPERTY
I am petitioning for a reduction of: ☐ Real Market Value (RMV) ☐ Assessed Value (AV)

	Real Market Value from Tax Statement or Assessor's Records	Real Market Value Requested by Petitioner	Assessed Value from Tax Statement or Assessor's Records	Assessed Value Requested by Petitioner
Land				
Improvement				
Mobile Home				
Total				

The following facts relate to the value of the property described above. (If your petition pertains to income producing property attach an income and expense statement for the current year and the past two or more years.)

Purchase price	Date of purchase	Terms: ☐ Cash ☐ Contract ☐ Trade ☐ Other

Has the property been offered for sale within the past two years? ☐ Yes ☐ No	When?	How long?	How offered?	Asking price

Was property appraised by someone other than assessor within the past two years? ☐ Yes ☐ No	Purpose and date of appraisal	Appraised by	Appraised value

List additions or improvements that have been made since purchase of the property:

Petitioner relies upon the following additional facts for the relief requested (attach additional pages if necessary):

DECLARATION

I understand the following:
- If this petition is incomplete or completed incorrectly, it will be returned.
- This petition will be heard at a board of equalization hearing and I may make additions or corrections to the petition up to and including the time of the hearing.
- If the petition does not contain the required information as of the time of the hearing, it will be dismissed.

I wish to be present or be represented at the hearing: ☐ Yes ☐ No

Address where hearing notification and decision is to be mailed:

Street		Phone No. — Day

City	State	ZIP Code	Phone No. — Evening

I declare under the penalties for false swearing (ORS 305.990(4)) that I have examined this document, and to the best of my knowledge, it is true, correct, and complete.

X _____

Signature of petitioner or petitioner's representative (attach power of attorney)	Date	Relationship to petitioner

INDEX

Index

ACKNOWLEDGMENTS

This book could not have been assembled without the cooperation of scores of property-tax administrators throughout the nation. Nor could it have been completed without the aid and encouragement of my personal critic, editor and wife, Luana Luther, and the publisher of Panoply Press, Heather Kibbey.

I also want to recognize the hundreds of public servants who, during my long career as a political writer, provided me with a wealth of information about the complex workings of local, state and federal government. Specifically, I want to thank those who have actually made my work in the tax-appeals process an enjoyable activity. These include my colleagues on the Clackamas County Board of Equalization, Chester Brooks and Kris Preslan; County Commissioners Darlene Hooley, Judie Hammerstad and Ed Lindquist; County Clerk, John Kauffmann, County Assessor Ray Erland and his assistant Bill Martin, and especially the Board of Equalization Clerk, Vicki Greenwood.

ABOUT THE AUTHOR

Ed Salzman was chosen to serve as a member of the Clackamas County Board of Equalization in Oregon following a 40-year career as a journalist specializing in government and politics. He is the author or co-author of several books, including the *Almanac of State Government and Politics*, *Jerry Brown: High Priest and Low Politician*, *California Public Administration*, and *The Cartoon History of California Politics*. During his journalistic career, he worked for the Boston Globe, Oakland Tribune, Sacramento Bee and several other newspapers. He was managing editor of America's first all-news radio station, editor of the California Journal magazine, and editor and publisher of Golden State Report magazine. He lives in Lake Oswego, Oregon.

Also by Ed Salzman:

Almanac of State Government and Politics
Jerry Brown: High Priest and Low Politician
California Public Administration (co-author)
The California Political Action Handbook
The Cartoon History of California Politics (co-author)
California Environment and Energy
California Governments and Politics Annual
    (co-author),1974-1983